WHERE  DO I GO FROM HERE?

JOHN TRENT Ph.D.
KARI TRENT STAGEBERG

LifeMapping® Your Way from
Personal Chaos to Purposeful Calm

FOCUS
ON THE FAMILY.

A Focus on the Family resource
published by Tyndale House Publishers

Everyone has dreams,
but not everyone
gets to live with one.

This book is lovingly dedicated to my wife, Cindy, who has been the
main supporting character in my life story for more than forty years.
Too many times to count, her prayers, love, and support have
steered me away from detours and rough roads and kept
me focused and on track. I thank God that my LifeMap
includes a life partner who is also my best friend.

CONTENTS

PART 1

The Benefits, Tools, and Process of LifeMapping®

CHAPTER 1

From Personal Chaos
to Purposeful Calm

BRIAN WAS TWENTY-FIVE years old, in shape, successful, in line for a promotion . . . and ready to give up on life.

So much in his life story had been pushed back: dating and marriage, friendships, and joining others in running those 5Ks and half marathons he loved doing. So, too, had travel for work or any kind of fun escape trip. He'd had to remain physically disconnected from his family, who were all out of state—now for going on *three years*.

Brian had lived alone for the entire pandemic, doing his work by computer. He'd also followed every changing and challenging mandate that his "let's take this seriously" state had issued. He followed those edicts regarding masks and vaccinations, boosters and eating out, as well as pushing back anything that seemed like a normal life gathering. He didn't realize that like so many, he was now experiencing trickle-down anxiety and depression that were eating away at his view of relationships and life.[1]

Strangely, the more Zoom meetings and FaceTime chats he had online, the less he felt like actually meeting with others face-to-face. Even when places began to reopen, he was reluctant to pursue real relationships. Cut off from satisfying that deep need for connection with others for so long, screen relationships seemed safer. But he discovered what so many had—that online connections were like trying to eat an imaginary meal. It might be a beautiful 3D picture of the real thing, but such connections are as emotionally cold and unfulfilling as the glass screen he looks through.

Toss in all the constant, dramatic changes in culture he was trying to keep up with, plus the persistent calls for dramatic climate measures that demanded the world make massive changes to the way people lived life *now*. And the result?

Brian hadn't taken part in the *Lancet* medical journal survey of more than ten thousand young people ages sixteen to twenty-five done in 2021.[2] However, had he taken it, he would have agreed with the 75 percent of respondents who said they thought "the future is frightening." He also would have concurred with the 50 percent who felt that regardless of what anyone did, it was too late to matter. And he especially (and tragically) would have agreed with the 56 percent of young men and women who answered the question *What do you think of the future?* with this response: "Humanity is doomed."

In other words, why bother with connection, human caring, or any kind of life planning? Who cares about dating or mapping out the future or a meaningful career or doing something called LifeMapping? If there's no future, no hope, no purpose in the life behind you or any positive place to aim in front of you—if the world will soon be uninhabitable—then why bother even trying to answer the question *Where do I go from here?*

■

While all of us have been scared by the pandemic in ways large or small, Mary was a far different COVID casualty. All during the lockdown months, she always thought she was headed toward a positive future. After all, she had grown up in a Christian home.

Mary had gone to a Christian grade school and high school. In high school, she fell in love with a wonderful young man. The two of them managed to go to the same college, kept dating just each other, and graduated in four years. All that was capped off by them getting married two days after graduation, pledging their lives and futures to each other.

Mary had earned a degree in nursing, and her husband received one in civil engineering. They both found good jobs quickly, and they began to fill a nice apartment with special finds from fun weekend trips to local farmers markets and antique fairs. After their first anniversary, they even had their first serious conversation about whether their current apartment were too small—if *perhaps* down the road in a year or two they would start their family.

It was that conversation about launching their family that caused so much confusion for Mary—it was confusing, that is, in light of what happened soon after.

On the day her future disappeared, Mary's mind

went back to their first anniversary trip. They'd gone to Disneyland as a special celebration. One ride for which they'd waited patiently in a long line had for years been called the Tower of Terror. Now it was updated to feature characters from the movie *Guardians of the Galaxy*. That ride came to Mary's mind when she got home from her thirteen-hour nursing shift and found the note propped up on the kitchen table.

The handwritten note was from her husband. As she read it, she felt her heart and life go into free fall, like that massive drop in the *Guardians of the Galaxy* ride. The two of them had taken that fall together. But now she was doing it alone and in real life. The note told her that her husband was gone and would not be coming back.

There had been no telegraphing of his plans. No discussion. The note said he already had a lawyer. He was filing for divorce. He emphasized there would be no counseling.

He made clear that he was unwilling to meet with either of their parents or anyone on "her side." And absolutely no way was he going to meet with their pastor. He insisted he hadn't given up on his faith. Just on her.

Over the next year, until their divorce was finalized, he followed through on every aspect of that terrible note. His only contact was an occasional necessary email or text or an even rarer phone call—and, of course, that final face-to-face meeting in front of a judge. Mary's life had crashed down to rest on a future she would never, ever have imagined or picked out for herself. She took every extra shift at work to keep her mind busy, and so she came home too worn out to think. But every day, as she drove home—in fact, anytime she got five minutes to herself—she was bombarded by that question: *Where do I go from here?*

■

Lucia was the first in her family to finish college. Apart from at her quinceañera, when she'd turned fifteen, she had never seen her father act so proud or affectionate toward her as he had at her graduation, when she'd earned a counseling degree. Now she was finishing her clinical hours on her way to getting her counseling license. She'd just become a certified life coach as well.

Drawing from her own life story, she was helping first-generation immigrant parents bridge that huge gap between their birth culture and American culture. She was also coaching them to help their older children figure out what direction *their* lives could go in this land still filled with opportunities, despite all the challenges.

Lucia's life-coaching skills included a certification[3] in LifeMapping, which had helped her build out her own plan for the future. And now that map had become her go-to tool as she mentored others trying to deal with so many changes. She was helping each of them capture and celebrate their own life story while also guiding them to make sense of and build out a positive, prayed-over, realistic plan to face the myriad changes looming in the future.

■

Three lives. Three stories of people either experiencing massive change themselves or helping others deal with an unshakable sense of personal chaos caused by those un-expected changes that can hit us all.

The cover of this book is so well put together, it might seem like the subtitle of the book is incongruous or out of place: *LifeMapping Your Way from Personal Chaos to Purposeful Calm*. But even without all the "forced choice" changes we're dealing with in our post-pandemic-challenged world, life for most of us *will* have us taking a jour-ney through personal chaos at some point. Even if things have gone well for us and our loved ones so far, there will be a period of chaos that can cloud any view of a positive future.

Life for most of us *will* have us taking a journey through personal chaos at some point.

But while chaos is now almost universal, what's optional is the "calm" part. And that's what prompted the writing of this book.

For some, like Brian, personal chaos came from being pushed away from others, as well as being pulled by almost every fear-inducing headline and news story. All meshed together, the inner turmoil acted like an eraser, rubbing out any sense of stability, connection, or a positive future. It was as if he were living in a house of mirrors; any direction Brian looked, the reflection looking back was distorted or frightening.

For many of us, the unmet needs of having both someone to keep us sane and something to look forward to can lead us to feel life is empty. Hopeless. Pointless. Or in Brian's case, even worse. Perhaps you or a loved one can relate to Brian.

Or perhaps, like Mary, you've picked up this book because unwanted or at least unexpected changes have crashed into your life. Perhaps, as with Mary, those changes have shattered dreams and broken trust. They've been one of life's terrible sucker punches you never saw coming. You've suffered the loss of a future you didn't even know was in danger. When something like that happens, it can freeze your heart and cloud your future, forcing you to answer the question you don't want to answer but now must: *Where do I go from here?*

Or perhaps, like Lucia, you're at a place in your life where that question doesn't seem so fearful or uncertain. You've built out a genuine plan for a future that really is possible. It's a reality-based plan that is biblical, practical, and hopeful. It helps you deal with past hurts while also laying out positive mile markers for what you believe will be a life well lived. Now you're looking to master the process so you can be of significant help to others.

Those are just three stories and three reasons we believe this book and life-directing tool can make a huge difference in your life. Like putting on your own oxygen mask first on an airplane, this book can and should be of help to you first. But it will also equip you to help others find confidence, courage, and resilience as they map out their own positive life plans.

It is simply amazing to see the scales of chaos drop from a person's eyes. To see someone blinded by pain, loss, and negative change gain some clarity and personal calm, in part by showing the person how you've done that in your own life.

In this book, you're going to learn about a life-giving, life-changing tool called LifeMapping. It will be the main tool we use in helping make that transition from personal chaos to purposeful calm.

It's a strengths-based, future-focused tool that has helped thousands of people see the key pieces of their life stories in a specific way—one that neither ignores nor minimizes the significant challenges someone has faced nor sugarcoats the huge issues facing us as a culture today. Yet this tool is able to help people move toward a place full of connection, caring, and calm instead of remaining stuck in isolation, loneliness, and chaos.

If that sounds like a journey you'd like to take—from personal chaos to purposeful calm—let's start with a definition of what we mean by LifeMapping.

CHAPTER 2

What Is LifeMapping®?

You're about to learn and begin using one of the most powerful tools we've ever seen for building personal character, facing powerful challenges, planning a promising future, and developing loving relationships. It's as old and wise as the Hebrew kings, as creative as Leonardo da Vinci and Walt Disney, and as contemporary as our nuclear-warship and Space Force programs.

It involves looking at your life—in all its component parts—in a new, fresh way. And it holds the promise of moving away from negative patterns and toward the intimacy, purpose, and direction you've always wanted, a way of living that gives you handrails for being loved by—and loving like—Jesus.

While we'll explain in more detail the key elements of LifeMapping, let's start with a simple definition:

> *LifeMapping* is a way of looking at your life by displaying its key component parts so that you see crucial events, positive and negative patterns, and your full potential in a fresh, new way. It involves storyboarding your past and your future so that you become an active participant in celebrating and rewriting parts of your life story. And its goal is to move you with clarity and conviction, starting today, toward closer relationships, Christlikeness, and a hope-filled future.

Six Reasons LifeMapping Can Be So Helpful

1. LifeMapping is a strengths-based, future-focused process.

In a world filled with people saying the future is bleak, there is another voice we can listen to. It's the voice of Him who called the world into being and said of its future, "'For I know the plans that I have for you,' declares the LORD, 'plans for prosperity and not for disaster, to give you a future and a hope'" (Jeremiah 29:11).

Those encouraging words from the prophet Jeremiah were given to a group of struggling exiles who had lost everything. As far as they knew, there was nothing but death in front of them. In those very worst of times for God's people, the light of God's Word shone like a lantern set out at dusk by a high mountain hut keeper. That light shines brighter as the world becomes darker, drawing climbers out of the darkness and cold and into a place of warmth and rest.

As such, LifeMapping is a solution-oriented process that seeks to uncover a person's God-given strengths. What's more, while it encourages men and women to gain insight from their past, it's based on setting clear goals and plans with a strong hope for the future.

In fact, that process is the very thing that helped Brian swerve away from hopelessness and final despair.

When Brian (pushed by a caring friend) came in for counseling, he was fresh out of options, with almost every mental shelf cleaned out of hope. But in the action-oriented, strengths-based, solution-focused approach of LifeMapping, he was able to graphically picture both his struggles and his strengths. He also had his eyes opened to the fact that God isn't finished with our world yet—nor with him. No matter how dire the headlines demanding despair were, Brian rapidly began working toward a solution instead of planning an ending.

Focusing on strengths, solutions, and a hopeful future in LifeMapping can be different from some counseling approaches. For many people looking for help, the only focus is on the past. That means they step back into recovery—but may never move forward and recover! Brian needed more than a single-focus approach (looking back). He needed a life picture like the one he built in the LifeMapping process that made such a difference, because it helped him make a plan for his future.

2. LifeMapping gives a person a graphic picture of the key events of his or her goals and life story.

Mary, whom we met earlier, was another person who drew a blank when it came to picturing a positive future after seeing her life story blow up. The dark clouds in her life reflected the inner hurt King Solomon wrote about: "Remember also your Creator . . . before the evil days come and the years approach when you will say, 'I have no pleasure in them'; before the sun and the light, the moon and the stars are darkened, and clouds return after the rain" (Ecclesiastes 12:1-2).

What an image of despair and darkness! Mary's loneliness, confusion, and discouragement seemed to drape over her like an endless winter. Attending a divorce recovery workshop at her church, where everyone was required to do a LifeMap, helped Mary realize for the first time that there was still a future in front of her.

"It was really hard at first," she wrote. "I sat there for the longest time looking at the 'strengths' section, drawing nothing but a blank. But I ran out of cards under the 'freeze point' section. As bad as that was, for the first time I saw right before me that those negative memories were only one part of me. There was still a whole LifeMap to build out. That one thing helped me see I did have a future. And *that* I could do something about. That day, I made a decision to plan out a new direction where I could use my strengths to serve God."

Things began to turn around for Mary when she finally got a picture of her life story. In confronting the good and the bad, her personal triumphs and shattered dreams all laid out before her, she could finally see rays of God's light breaking through. Jesus had been with her all the time, though her trials had clouded that fact for quite a while. The picture of her life story helped her see more clearly His presence in her life. And what's more, it ignited a resolve to make positive changes and to begin to plan again a different, hopeful outcome.

As Gary Smalley and I (John Trent) described in our book *The Language of Love*, pictures are incredibly powerful tools when employed in our relationships. LifeMapping derives much of its impact from helping people get a picture of their life story.

Technically, LifeMapping does this by utilizing something I call *incremental visual display learning*. That's a term that may seem long and confusing enough to be on a government form, but it's easy to grasp if we break it down.

It's *incremental* because it employs a step-by-step process to help a person put the pieces of his or her life story together. And the process of creating a LifeMap uses *visual* reminders to capture key life events, giving people a graphic *display* of who they are and what they can become. LifeMapping also draws deeply from a third well—biblical optimism.

3. LifeMapping is grounded in authentic, biblical optimism.

Consider the example of Henry, who struggled with an anemic spiritual life. It's not that he didn't want to grow spiritually, but his ups and downs made him feel like a poster child for Romans 7:18, 24: "For the willing is present in me, but the doing of the good is not. . . . Wretched man that I am!"

Henry operated the way many people do. His spiritual life was only as good as the last seminar or inspiring message he had heard. In fact, even those few spikes of spiritual attention seemed to vanish between the pew and the parking lot. Or, put another way, it was as if he was always running on empty. Each trip to church or Bible study gave him enough fuel for the moment—but then he was stuck and stopped again.

That's why the most exciting part of LifeMapping to him was gaining an increased sense of personal control. Rooted in that growing sense of motivation and self-discipline he experienced a hearty dose of biblical optimism. Not the kind of optimism that Pollyanna practiced. ("Oh, you broke your leg? How wonderful!") Rather, he had biblical optimism, a choice of perspective that convinced him he had all the God-given tools he needed to do something positive about his spiritual life.

Genuine optimism always leads to action. It's optimism's opposite, hopelessness, that bogs down many of us and robs us of great relationships. In shedding that driftwood syndrome he was stuck in, Henry finally stopped wandering spiritually and set a clear course toward Christlikeness.

4. LifeMapping can help you move away from past hurts.

Would you like to be able to rewrite your life story? Would you like to turn around negative patterns from your past and replace them with a whole new, loving attitude?

If so, you're not alone. All of us have pages or entire chapters in our lives that we'd like to rewrite—even tear out. And many of us fear something even worse. Namely, we're afraid that the pain we've experienced will be forged in steel and we'll never be free of it—a terrible set of chains laid on us that we, in turn, will forge for our children.

As you carefully read the words that follow (my paraphrase of a famous story), try to remember where you've heard or seen the tale. It was written nearly two hundred years ago by a man deeply influenced by the Scriptures. And ever since, it has given us a powerful word picture of a biblical truth: We can change the ultimate outcome of our lives.[1]

It's after midnight on a ghastly winter night. The rain comes down in sheets on the shivering form of a broken man. His unwanted companion is not a man but a horrible ghost—a frightening, black-robed monster made more terrible by his unwillingness to speak a single word.

Finally, the spirit points his long skeleton finger at a nondescript headstone, forcing the anguished man to look through the rain at the letters etched in granite.

"Before I draw nearer to that stone to which you point," the man begs, "answer me one question. Are these the shadows of the things that *will* be, or are they shadows of things that *may* be?"

Still, the ghost refuses to reply and points menacingly toward the nearby grave.

"The course of a man's life will determine its ends; I know that," the man says. "If he perseveres in that direction, that's where it must lead. *But if that man changes course, the ends will change, won't they? Won't they?*"

Suddenly, an explosion of lightning bathes the graveyard in chalk-white light, illuminating the headstone just long enough for him to read what's written. With a choked scream, the man falls back in uncontrollable terror! It's *his* name on the stone. His death recorded. His life ended without remorse or regret by anyone who knew him!

"Spirit!" he cries, clutching tightly to the specter's robe. "Hear me! I am not the man I was! Assure me that I yet may change these shadows you have shown me by an altered life!"

For the first time, the cold steel that had been the ghost's demeanor begins to change. Instead of an iron will, the bony hand appears to shake.

Sensing there is still a chance, the man cries out, "I will honor Christmas in my heart and try to keep it all the year. I will live in the past, the present, and the future. The spirits of all three shall strive within me. I will not shut out the lessons that they teach.

"Oh, tell me I may sponge away the writing on this stone!"

Sound familiar? By now, I'm sure you've guessed that this scene comes from Charles Dickens's classic *A Christmas Carol*, featuring Ebenezer Scrooge. Since it was first published, Scrooge's story has been a holiday favorite performed by Shakespearean troupes, high school drama departments, and even the Muppets!

There's a reason so many are drawn to this story again and again. Namely, Scrooge's cry is often our own.

"Oh, tell me I may sponge away the writing on this stone!"

One powerful element of the LifeMapping process is its ability to help you identify and begin to move past a hurtful history—not by ignoring difficult issues or minimizing their pain or potential consequences but by appropriating the life-changing power of God's Spirit to redirect a life. To rewrite a life story. To draw a LifeMap to a better tomorrow.

With God's help, we can sponge away the crippling pain of harmful actions and outcomes. Pictures of a negative future that others may have predicted for us can lose their power to be carved in stone. That's because the Lord has already carved words of a special future for each of us, guaranteed by His love: "You are a letter of Christ . . . written not with ink but with the Spirit of the living God, not on tablets of stone but on tablets of human hearts" (2 Corinthians 3:3).

Everyone is influenced by his or her past. But as Christians, none of us has to be controlled by it. In the pages that follow, you'll learn specific tools to live a life free of chains, as well as how to free those around you to become all God intends them to be.

5. LifeMapping can move you toward a life-giving, hopeful future.

Have you ever felt that you were spinning your wheels, that you were merely existing, not contributing anything positive to God's Kingdom?

Or do you, in contrast, have a clear purpose that gets you up in the morning and inspires you to do your best all day long? Do you have a tangible, written plan, flexible to God's leading but pointing you forward in each major area of your life? Do you have a clearly defined direction that can keep you from seeing failures as final and mistakes as global?

Not only can LifeMapping help you move away from past hurts, but it also holds tremendous power to point you toward a positive, God-honoring future. Everyone needs a clear idea of where he or she is headed. In fact, if you don't have a positive plan for your future, you may well be putting your relational and physical health at risk.

"How?" you may ask.

It may seem there's no real cost to being aimless, but lack of purpose actually drains energy and life. Since that may sound like an exaggeration, let's look at a dramatic example.

> If you don't have a positive plan for your future, you may well be putting your relational and physical health at risk.

From 1942–45, Dr. Viktor Frankl was imprisoned in four different Nazi concentration camps, enduring the deaths of his parents, his brother, and his wife.

Frankl was a psychiatrist whom the Nazis forced to treat hurting people, despite having next to no medical supplies. While observing hundreds of fellow prisoners during those terrible years, he made a startling observation: People could live through even the most deplorable conditions as long as they had a clear purpose to hold on to. That purpose for living could be anything from planting another garden to holding a loved one's hand when they got out to finishing a piece of art. As long as prisoners felt they had some tangible goal to live for, they could tolerate incredible doses of emotional and physical trauma. *But once they lost their picture of a positive future, it wasn't long before their lives were at risk.*

"It is a peculiarity of man that he can only live by looking to the future," wrote Frankl. "Woe to him who saw no more sense in his life, no aim, no purpose and therefore no point in carrying on. He was soon lost."

Frankl told the story of a fellow prisoner, a well-known composer, who had confided to him a particularly vivid dream he'd had. In the dream, the man felt certain that he'd been given a gift by a special voice. That voice had whispered the exact day their camp would be liberated and their sufferings would come to an end. The date: March 30, 1945.

When that man told Frankl about his dream, he was full of hope and conviction that the voice would be right. But as the promised day drew nearer, the war news that reached the camp made it obvious that they wouldn't be free on that date.

On March 29, the man suddenly became ill and ran a high temperature.

On March 30, the day his prophecy had told him the war and his suffering would end, he became delirious and lost consciousness.

On March 31, he was dead.

Frankl surmised from that man's death, and countless others he observed as the camp doctor, that the cause was the absence of a man or woman's clear purpose. Conversely, a sense of the future sustained people through tough times.[2]

"Come on, Trent," you may want to say. "Are you really suggesting that having a clear plan for the future is a life-and-death issue? What about all those couch potatoes whose only 'life plan' is binging on this week's podcast or streaming series?"

In the Scriptures, the word for a couch potato is *sluggard.* And while the lack of purpose, energy, and direction in such people may make it look as though they're enjoying a life of leisure, their lives may actually be full of pain.

"'A little sleep, a little slumber, a little folding of the hands to rest,' then your poverty will come in like a drifter, and your need like an armed man" (Proverbs 6:10-11).

Sluggards may be wonderful people, but they're storing up potential pain. We need to realize that on a personal level, we're either moving forward or falling back. The same thing is true in our spiritual lives.

A primary key to living a fulfilling, contributing, Christlike life is to focus on the future. We're told to look forward to the blessed hope of Jesus' return and "a new heaven and a new earth" God has promised (Revelation 21:1). Like it or not, how clearly we picture our future, both spiritually and physically, will directly affect our quality of life—and often its length as well!

God has a very real plan for each of us, young and old. And as you flesh out that plan in your unique life setting—and help others do so as well—you'll discover its power to bring important, life-giving changes to your spheres of influence.

6. LifeMapping can provide major motivation toward Christlikeness.

Thus far, we've seen how LifeMapping can help you personally and with your close relationships. But perhaps its greatest value is in freeing you to come closer to your heavenly Father.

As you look at the component parts of your life and put them into a clearly laid-out plan, you'll begin to see more than just the individual parts. You'll soon start to see connections and transitions, dead stops and new beginnings, major decisions and potential memorial markers that were all directed by the hand of God. You'll understand that you're on a journey through life so profound and so personal that your daily actions count, and the very hairs on your head are counted.

In the pages that follow, you'll also see that it's the Author of happy endings who wants you and me to have fulfilling lives, a purpose that matches His own for us, and a plan right out of Scripture that can make our lives into living examples of the love of God.

That's what Rich needed to know in the worst way.

Rich wasn't a Wayne Gretzky or a Bobby Hull when it came to hockey, but he had the talent to be drafted by the NHL. That is, until he took just one run on a family ski trip, caught an edge, and kissed his left knee goodbye.

Few of us have to face the instantaneous, 180-degree career and dream change forced upon Rich by a single ski run. He immediately went from being a pro prospect to being grateful he could walk and slowly jog. And despite his best efforts at rehabilitation, Rich would never get beyond doing well just to keep up with his family at a skating rink.

When life goes from full speed ahead to dead stop in a matter of moments, it can put tremendous strain on our personal, marital, and spiritual lives. Rich initially responded to that stress by eating his feelings and adding nearly forty pounds to his body. He struggled daily with self-doubt. For many athletes, the older they get, the better they are in their imaginations. But for Rich, he didn't just imagine himself to be really good. His shot at the pros had been real. And he woke up day after day shaking his head (or his fist) at the "stupidity" that caused him to toss away a career he had aspired to since he was six years old.

Part of Rich's healing came when everyone in his small group at church decided to go through the LifeMapping process. As he looked at the flash point that upended everything in his life, he suddenly saw how God's hand had been an ever-present part of his life story. The Lord hadn't thundered at him that changes were needed, but as Rich storyboarded the key ups and downs of his life, the sum of the parts seen all together took on a whole new shape. In sharing his LifeMap with his small group, it suddenly became obvious to him that God was an author of happy endings, even if Rich's wasn't the ending Rich had predicted for himself.

As it was for Henry and for Rich, LifeMapping can be a great aid to your daily life, especially in the following ways:

- Spending time well
- Dealing effectively with the past
- Gaining a clear plan for the future
- Improving communication and problem solving
- Adding intimacy while reducing daily stress
- Deepening your spiritual life

Sounds like the lead-in to an infomercial or a speech by someone running for elective office, doesn't it? But those are all tangible reasons and results of your investment of time, energy, and accountability in the LifeMapping process. What's more, after you've finished your LifeMap, just lift your eyes to see those in your family, friendships, neighborhood, or workplace—so many people who need your help to get unstuck and move toward health and life as well!

Are you ready to look at the LifeMapping tool itself? Good. In our crazy online world, there are a thousand ways to waste time. But not even one minute of time will ever be a waste when spent in building up your personal and spiritual life—or in helping others do the same.

CHAPTER 3

How LifeMapping® Began

WE'VE TALKED ABOUT the need to move from personal chaos to purposeful calm. We've defined *LifeMapping* and talked about six ways it can be of significant help in your own life and for those you look to encourage.

In this chapter, I (John) will explain where LifeMapping came from. To really understand something (or someone), it's important to understand its background. That's certainly true with LifeMapping. As you'll see, God used two things to open my eyes to first see and then create the LifeMapping tool.

How Missing Key Parts of a Story Led to a Tool Able to Capture a Life Story

I'll forever be grateful to Northwest Bible Church in Dallas, Texas. Years ago, they not only hired me as their minister to families, but they also invested in me by sending me to school to get my doctorate in counseling. The problem was that, although counseling was my major, I was struggling to help people who were stuck. It wasn't for lack of prayer or trying or studying for my classes. I was struggling to carve an inroad into these people's lives that could get them moving in a different, more positive direction.

No one I was seeing had signed up to have a terrible marriage. But that's where they were. No individual had set a goal to be stuck in depression or shame or to be filled with anxiety. Yet it was as if at some point, each one had reached a dead end and was now unable to get out or get back on the road to fullness of life.

Even as I tried to help, I kept feeling like I was missing out on key parts of their stories. It wasn't just casual insights I needed but information about key events and decisions that one or both spouses had made, perhaps decades before we'd met. I could tell significant incidents had taken place and were clearly affecting their current relationships. It was as if we kept tripping over invisible lines and barriers in the counseling room that I couldn't see and didn't know how to draw out.

That's when two things happened in a short period of time that helped me finally begin to understand more about those I was counseling.

First, I started a study in the biblical book of Revelation. That may not seem like the best place to look for counseling tools. However, I hadn't gone far—just to chapter 2—when I saw something that described what I was seeing in many of the couples and individuals I was meeting with each day. It also provided insight into why I wasn't really helping them.

For some context: Chapter 1 of Revelation gives us a wonderful picture of the resurrected Lord Jesus in all His heavenly light and glory. Then chapter 2 gives us a picture of Jesus walking among, or looking at, seven different churches and commenting on them. The first of these churches was the church in Ephesus.

Long story short, at first glance, of the seven churches talked about in Revelation, you definitely would've wanted your membership to be in this first church. According to Jesus, these people were spiritual rock stars. Seven times He praised them. (In Scripture, the number seven signifies completion or fulfillment.) In our world, we'd say they were killing it. They'd been there, done that, and gotten the "We're the best" T-shirt. They'd been faithful and discerning. Courageous and caring. Yet those were the things they *had* been. Jesus told them how well they'd done, but then He told them who and where they were *today*.

"But I have *this* against you, that you have left your first love" (Revelation 2:4).

Thinking back to my struggling counseling sessions, I realized that this was what I was seeing in so many cases: wonderful, God-honoring people, many of whom had done positive things in life or in their marriages, some for years and years on end. But now I was seeing them at a very different time and in a very different light. What had happened?

I studied the phrase "left your first love" and discovered that it is a nautical image. The picture is of something that has happened slowly, even going unnoticed at first. The Ephesians were like a small boat that had been tied to a pier, but the rocking of the water loosened and finally untied the poorly tied knot, and the boat slowly drifted away. Where the Ephesian

Christians were now wasn't where they had started out. In leaving, they had drifted away.

Now those on board have woken up to realize there's no longer a safe haven or harbor surrounding them. They're in deep water and in a position to lose a lot: that first love. Their ability to shine light and impact others. I was seeing people at critical points in their life stories. Like the members of the church in Ephesus, they'd reached a *Where do I go from here?* point.

For the church in Ephesus, this moment was when Jesus shared with them a pathway back to love and purpose. To connection and caring. To security and safety. To following the light and getting back to being a light to others as well. And He did so by telling them three things.

First, "Remember from where you have fallen" (Revelation 2:5).

More than one hundred times in Scripture, we're told to "remember," "remember," "remember . . ." But in this particular verse, the message is for those who have ended up in a place they don't want to be. Jesus provided an amazingly succinct, clear way back to a place they wanted to be yet couldn't find on their own.

If you come from a background of legalism or a lack of love, it would be easy to think that Jesus, as some faraway authority figure who points out that we're in trouble, wants to add shame and loss to our hurt.

But look back at what Jesus actually said.

He wasn't interested in shaming or blaming them.

He was interested in helping them answer the question *Where do I go from here?*

And His answer came in three parts. The first: "Remember from where you have fallen."

That shocked me. *You do not fall from the lowest place in your life.*

That's where the people who were sitting in my office had found themselves. They could talk for hours about all the negatives—and I was letting them. But Jesus sees people who have drifted off and calls them to look up, not down!

These people had drifted away from the warmth, love, connection, caring, and purpose they'd once had. But Jesus doesn't call us to focus on all the low points in our lives, to drag out every terrible detail of loss, or to heap self-blame on ourselves. Nor does He—though He has the right to!—shame or blame us. Rather, He tells us to shine a light on the positive things we've already done—to look up at where we've fallen from, which was a high point. To remember the things—there were seven of them in the case of the Ephesian church—that we have done well.

> **Jesus sees people who have drifted off and calls them to look up, not down!**

Remembering brings back memories. And memories bring back feelings. And feelings bring back pictures. And pictures bring back more memories—not just of the positives (if we recall positive things) but also of the people who originally lifted us to the high places and celebrated with us when we were there.

This blew me away. I had been focusing on the negative. It is important to understand someone's hurt and brokenness; being honest about our hurts is part of counseling and of LifeMapping. But I was so focused on the negative that I was never really getting around to helping people look more closely at the positive, as Jesus instructed. And as we'll see in the chapter on strengths, when people are hurting, it's important to help them lift their eyes if real changes are to be made.

The second part of the road map Jesus gave the Ephesian church to get back to light and love was "repent" (Revelation 2:5). Theologically, that's a powerful word. It literally means "to turn around." We're to quit walking into the water that's getting deeper with each step. (That water isn't going to somehow get shallower!) We're to have the wisdom and humility to drop our pride and admit we need to go in a different direction and to ask for forgiveness, if needed, for choosing to go the wrong way. But most of all, to repent isn't just an attitude—it's an *action*.

We're not meant to stay where we are. We need to be honest about where we've ended up, like the Prodigal Son (see Luke 15:11-32). Or if life has unfairly knocked us into the middle of a river, we must admit that that's where we are.

Dr. Deborah Gorton's outstanding book *Embracing Uncomfortable* comes to mind. There she talks about how people have to get comfortable being uncomfortable if they are to change.[1] Repentance requires admitting where we are, which is uncomfortable. But if we're stuck in the middle of the river, it does no good to stay there and worry about how we got there, how deep the water is, or what might bump into us. We need to turn around and swim back to shore. Then we need to get out, dry off, and start taking steps in a more positive direction.

But what direction?

Where do I go from here?

Jesus answered this in the third thing He called the Ephesian church to do: "Do the deeds you did at first" (Revelation 2:5).

This step requires that we think through what we did that worked well when we were living out that "first love"—when we were experiencing Jesus' love and loving others the way He does.

What were we doing that was helpful to ourselves and others? What was beneficial? Brave? Resilient? Caring? We could begin by listing the fruit of the Spirit (see Galatians 5:22-23). What were we doing that made us more loving, joyful, peaceful, patient, kind, and so on? It may have been a long time since we were living lives of honor, courage, and love. Regardless, Jesus calls us to look at what was happening before we drifted away.

All this will lead to thinking through and then laying out a plan for doing positive things once again. Not to save us—Jesus' blood and righteousness do that. Nor to strive for perfection, which just leads to unending, exhausting effort. Rather, we are called to get back to the freedom of our first-love zeal—to that time when we didn't even need a plan or mile markers or sheet music to play. It seemed so easy back then, didn't it? But the fact is that we live in a fallen, broken world. Black clouds gather, and we can lose our way. We can easily drift away and start acting like the opposite of what we want to be or used to be. (Read Romans 7:14-25 to see that struggle.)

Professional athletes have playbooks they're asked to study and memorize. They practice running the plays correctly over and over. Then, when a game starts, because of their great plan and frequent practice, they have the freedom to play their best. Amazingly, in real life, with a great plan and intentionality in focusing on the strengths and gifts God has given us comes the freedom to use our backgrounds and present skills to play with reckless abandon—to live out verses like "you will know the truth, and the truth will set you free" (John 8:32) and "I came so that they would have life, and have it abundantly" (John 10:10).

I realized that if the people I was seeking to help could see not just the negatives but also the positives of their life stories, they could begin to find their way back to each other, to the Lord, and to a way of doing life that blessed their children and freed them to serve and love others well.

But then, as suddenly as I had seen all this, I crashed back to earth.

How in the world can I help someone capture something as big as their whole life story? How could we encompass the high points as well as all their struggles and hurts—the many things they'd need to see in order to be honest about where they'd been and where they were today? They'd need to do all this so they could turn around and make a new life plan that would link the future with the positive things that had worked before.

There could be hundreds of pieces. I thought, *There's no way to do that.*

This led to the second thing that laid the foundation for LifeMapping, which was a knock on my door that brought an invitation that would take me to the tool powerful enough to capture even something as big as the conglomeration of all the pieces of someone's life story.

From Leonardo da Vinci to Disney
to a LifeMap for Those Who Are Lost

Let's go back to Northwest Bible Church. After studying what Jesus called the church in Ephesus to do, I better understood why the people who came to me for help were stuck and how they may have gotten off course. I realized that many people are thrown for a loop by life's challenges (like COVID) and wake up wondering, *Where do I go from here?* But there are also countless people who wake up one day, even after doing a lot of good for a long time, and find that they have drifted away. They've left the joy and attachment they once had, and they long to get it back, just as the church in Ephesus was called to.

It was while I was thinking about this one day that the knock came on my office door. And with it came the discovery of a tool dynamic and big enough to capture the key pieces of a person's life story! Here's how it happened.

"Hey, John. I've knocked on everyone else's door. They're either gone or busy. Any chance you could leave right now and go to a creativity seminar with me?"

I was brand new to the church, but I still knew the person who had stepped into my office. His name was Jack Turpin, and he was a hugely successful businessman in Dallas who attended the church. I knew he was on the board of Dallas Theological Seminary, where I'd gotten my master's degree. My wife, Cindy, and I had met his wife, Sally, at church.

I jumped at the chance. As we drove downtown, Jack told me he had paid a lot of money for him and someone in his office to go to this business seminar. Unfortunately, the man he'd planned to take had gotten sick.

What I didn't realize was how the Lord was going to change my life that afternoon.

Jack explained that we were going to a creativity seminar being taught in part by one of Disney's Nine Old Men. Among its members were key contributors to titles from *Steamboat Willie* to *Snow White and the Seven Dwarfs, Bambi,* and *Fantasia.*

What we learned when we got there was that a tool called *storyboarding* had come out of their getting stuck. Remember, there were no computers when the first animated cartoon was being made in 1928. There were no programs that could create an animation in moments then. These were the people who had brought animation to life!

As the "Old Man" began to talk about how storyboarding came about, I recognized that it was a tool dynamic and powerful enough to capture hundreds of pieces—and help turn them into a masterpiece!

The problem they'd had in 1928 was the very problem I was having. Remember, I was wondering how I could help those counselees who were stuck trying to answer the question *Where do I go from here?* As the "Old Man" began to talk about how storyboarding came about, I recognized that it was a tool dynamic and powerful enough to capture hundreds of pieces—and help turn them into a masterpiece!

It started with the great group of artists working to create the hundreds and hundreds of individual art cels—literal art pieces, each roughly 8½ × 11 inches—that would tell the story of Steamboat Willie. The artists were getting lost in trying to sequence (or edit) all these pieces.

They were about ready to give up when Walt Disney remembered something the famous artist Leonardo da Vinci had done years earlier using sketches and drawings: storyboarding.[2] Disney jumped into action and rented a warehouse in Garden Grove, California. There the animators took all the pieces of the story and put them up on the walls around them. Now they could see the beginning, the middle, and the end of the story all at once, and they could move the cels around as needed to put them in the right order. They'd found a way to capture all the pieces and turn them into a coherent story![3]

Storyboarding would become a tool that Walt Disney would use for all his cartoons and movies. Later, it would also be the creative foundation of Disneyland and Disney World. It's a skill still taught today at the Disney Institute.

On that day years ago, as I saw the speaker laying out pictures to tell a story, my jaw dropped. There it was: a creative tool that could take all the key pieces of a person's life story and capture them in a way that made sense. Not being able to draw, I realized that what I wanted to capture would be key *words* that make up key *word pictures* of someone's life. This process could organize the story not just of their past but also of where they are today and, prayerfully, where they could go toward God's best in the future.

That's why you're going to be using storyboarding when we dive into building your LifeMap. You won't be laying out literal pictures like Walt Disney or modern moviemakers, but the basic techniques that Disney used all those years ago are the same ones we'll use to storyboard your life. So keep reading, and we'll take a closer look at this amazing tool.

CHAPTER 4

The Storyboarding Tool

THIS CHAPTER WILL PROVIDE an overview of the entire LifeMapping process that you'll soon be experiencing. You'll begin to see terms like *"high hill" people, emotional freeze points, individual flash points, image management, learned hopefulness,* and *memorial markers.* These terms may sound new or confusing at first. But they'll soon make sense as we introduce all eight key LifeMapping elements here and then add much more detail in subsequent chapters.

The two of us teach whole classes at StrongFamilies.com on how teams, businesses, churches, military units, entrepreneurs, and ministries can use storyboarding to capture a huge idea or concept. We help people come up with the many pieces that can make their idea into a reality and lay those pieces out in a way they (and their team) can see the whole project before them.

In our version of storyboarding, all the key pieces of your LifeMap will fit into one of three categories: topic card, topper cards, and subber cards.

First, picture you're laying out your LifeMap. Let's go old school and say you've got several packets of 4 × 6 cards. You're going to use one card for each thought or idea. This begins with a card at the very top called your topic card. It will have your name, and it will say, for example, "John Trent's LifeMap."

John Trent's LIFEMAP

Right under the topic card, you'll see there's a whole row of cards. These cards are called (very creatively) topper cards. When I'm storyboarding a book, for example, I'm taking an idea and laying out the key elements of that concept I want to expound on. All the toppers become chapter titles. With LifeMapping, I'm giving you the eight toppers you'll be developing. In just a moment, I'll explain more about all the toppers that will make up your LifeMap. But here are the first four so you get the idea of how they're laid out.

John Trent's LIFEMAP

| PURPOSE | STRENGTHS, SUCCESSES & "HIGH HILL" PEOPLE | EMOTIONAL FREEZE POINTS | INDIVIDUAL FLASH POINTS |

Then, under each of these toppers, you'll begin to develop what are called the subbers; they're subordinate to the toppers. For example, under the topper card Strengths, Successes, and "High Hill" People, you'll start populating (one on each card) key strengths, things you've accomplished, and people who were hugely important in your life in positive ways. Here's an example of subbers fleshed out under topper cards.

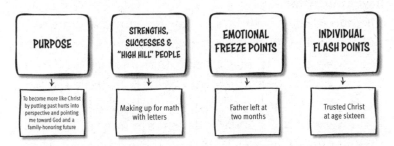

That's the gist of the tool. We'll spend the rest of this book learning how to use it to create your LifeMap. But if you want training on how to use storyboarding to build out almost anything—from a relatively stress-free camping trip to a successful household move to a book to a new business or ministry to a new tool or program or ministry outreach— we offer extra help at StrongFamilies.com/storyboarding.

While I didn't know it at the time of the seminar, Disney's style of storyboarding had already influenced many writers. If you Google "writers using storyboarding," you'll find pictures of Faulkner and Hemingway using storyboarding and of modern writers like J. K. Rowling mapping out the Harry Potter series.

As you can now see, on that day, I felt as if God had given me an incredible gift. This tool could take something as big as someone's life story and help draw out the key pieces, stories, and events. Then it could sequence them in a way that helped the person make sense of that three-part map back toward love, connection, and purpose that Jesus laid out in Revelation 2. It could help someone look back and see where they've been in a positive way. It could help them see what they needed to do today to repent, to turn around, from what isn't working and create a positive plan for a God-honoring future!

You can guess what I told my wife, Cindy, at dinner that night after the creativity workshop. And how I stayed up for hours that night, laying out that first LifeMap (my own). I was ready the next day when one of the couples I'd been struggling to help came in for counseling. They were the first ones who had a LifeMap laid out in front of them, and they were the first ones to lay out those key elements and aspects of their own life story. Where they'd been. Where they were today. What needed to change. And how they could begin to build a plan toward a more positive, God-honoring future.

There have been updates to that original LifeMap in the forty years since meeting with that first couple. Thankfully, it was a great help to them, and it's helped Kari and me help hundreds of people ever since. That includes the life coaches, counselors, and lay leaders we train today as LifeMapping coaches. And now it will also include you!

Let's look at today's version of the LifeMap that you'll be using to capture the key elements of your life story. Again, in storyboarding lingo, you'll be looking at toppers and subbers (or what I sometimes call *posts*; think of a 4 × 6 card with 3 × 5 cards under it). But what you'll see can help you picture what you'll be doing throughout this book.

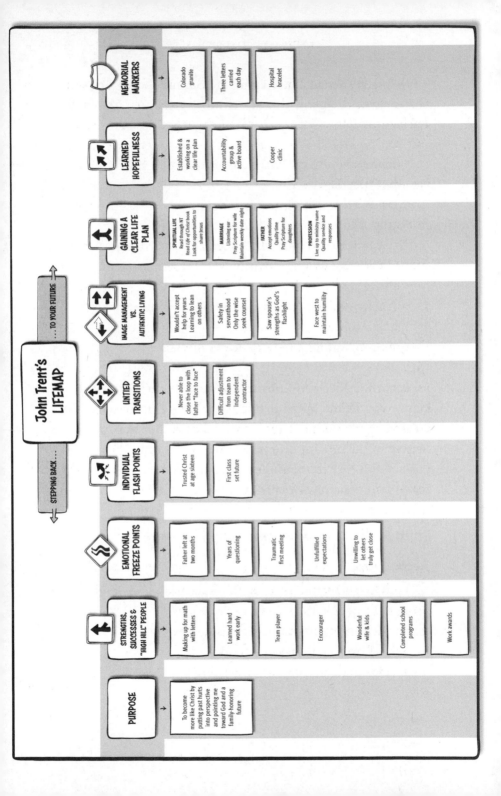

While my actual LifeMap includes more specifics or sub-bers in each category, this scaled-down example highlights the eight major elements that make up the process:

- Remembering your strengths, successes, and "high hill" people
- Uncovering emotional freeze points
- Understanding individual flash points
- Dealing with major, and especially untied, transitions
- Choosing authentic living over image management
- Planning a positive future
- Practicing learned hopefulness instead of learned helplessness
- Picking out tangible memorial markers

Eight LifeMapping components may seem like a lot. But before you throw up your hands and say, "I'm just not the creative, organized, reflective type," know that this tool will help draw out and capture your thoughts, dreams, hurts, and goals. With that in mind, let's take an overview of the eight major components of LifeMapping.

Eight Steps to Creating Your Own LifeMap

Stepping back . . .

1. Recognizing your strengths, successes, and "high hill" people
2. Identifying emotional freeze points
3. Uncovering individual flash points
4. Dealing with untied transitions

. . . to your future

5. Choosing authentic living over image management
6. Gaining a clear plan for your future
7. Practicing learned hopefulness
8. Lining up memorial markers for lasting change

We'll spend entire chapters on each of those key elements. But for now, let's begin with a brief introduction.

Stepping Back . . .

LifeMapping begins by looking back in a specific way. There's a consistent theme in Scripture wrapped around that often-repeated word *remember.*

"Remember also your Creator in the days of your youth" (Ecclesiastes 12:1). "Remember the former things long past, for I am God, and there is no other" (Isaiah 46:9).

But what, exactly, is God asking us to do? A key is found in the word picture behind this Old Testament word itself. In Hebrew, one meaning is to make an imprint of something. Think of an embossed piece of paper or a notary crimping a document with his seal. We're to think back on key events and times that have made an indelible mark on our lives.

That's the goal in the first four elements of LifeMapping— to remember and mark out your successes and failures. Those key events and important patterns. The dreams you saw realized and opportunities you missed that have shaped your past. And doing so begins by doing the following.

1. RECOGNIZING YOUR STRENGTHS, SUCCESSES, AND "HIGH HILL" PEOPLE

You wouldn't dream of beginning a cross-country trip without first checking the gas and oil levels of your car (at least if you were serious about arriving at your final destination). In our journey toward Christlikeness, the same thing ought to be true. We need to check three important internal levels as we begin the LifeMapping process.

First, each person has a deep, heartfelt, legitimate need to be loved and feel valuable, to know he or she is accepted by others. Our search for acceptance begins with our earliest caregivers. Then, as we mature, we look for deeper levels of acceptance in the eyes of a spouse and in the heart of a loving God. Are you running on empty when it comes to personal acceptance, or is there a deep knowledge of specific positive memories—imprints of unquestioned acceptance by important people we'll call *"high hill" people*?

If you've struggled in the area of personal relationships, internal motivation, or with truly feeling loved and forgiven by God, this first step in LifeMapping may help identify the impasse . . . and become the bridge you need to make positive changes.

This begins by clearly understanding your God-given strengths and successes. As Christians, we of all people should be aware of our spiritual giftedness and God-given strengths. However, I've found just the opposite to be true.

In talking with hundreds of believers across the country, I've found that many can come up with a list of their greatest weaknesses in seconds. But leap years would pass before they could list their three greatest strengths!

This first aspect of LifeMapping builds on the positive

and will help you to focus on the successes God has given you, big and little. In addition, you'll learn about your personal strengths and how understanding them can be a key factor in defeating your personal weaknesses. To help in this process, we use an online assessment called the Connect Assessment.

You'll find out how important it is to have as a part of your LifeMap those "high hill" people we mentioned that God placed in your life. Remember how memories bring back not just pictures but pictures of people in our mind's eye. In this case, we're making note of people who have lifted up and encouraged you in the past.

2. IDENTIFYING EMOTIONAL FREEZE POINTS

Spotlighting your personal strengths, successes, and "high hill" people can provide a positive directional sign in your journey toward Christlikeness. But the first warning sign we need to heed in the LifeMapping process is a concept we've called an *emotional freeze point.*

As we'll discuss later in more detail, an emotional freeze point comes out of a difficult season that you've gone through. While challenging times don't have to produce freeze points, they often do if they remain unprocessed and unexamined. When that happens, those feelings of anger, fear, or worry, laid down repeatedly over time, can form an inner layer of emotional ice. The result is to slow down or even stop completely the growth of mature, Christ-centered love.

A freeze point might have come from a nagging sense of worthlessness after trying and failing five times to get into graduate school. It may be the chilling fear of ever being dominated again by a high-control parent. Or it may be that defensive reflex that comes from three years of reporting to an alcoholic boss—someone who has made every working hour a nightmare.

As we look at emotional freeze points, you'll see how to identify them as well as ways of moving beyond them. And while a freeze point involves a season of time, there are also events in life that can change you for better or worse in the space between heartbeats.

3. UNCOVERING INDIVIDUAL FLASH POINTS

Some of us have experienced, like a lightning bolt out of a summer sky, a moment in time that has either pushed our lives backward or propelled them forward.

Those are *individual flash points*, and they can hit with the suddenness of a heart-stopping, unexpected thunderclap.

In some cases, it may have been a positive sound that rolled over you, such as "It's triplets!" Or it may have been the terrible sound of tearing metal in a crash that instantly changed your life. In either case, it was an unexpected, unplanned occurrence that dramatically shifted the direction of your life.

As you honestly appraise your past, it will be important to see if a flash point has affected the direction you've been heading ever since. In chapter 7, we'll look at a man named Saul whose brief encounter with a blinding light on the road to Damascus changed his life instantaneously and forever in a positive way. But there are also ways a flash point can push us back or cause us to shelter in place and vow to never risk (or love) again.

With this working knowledge of your strengths, successes, and "high hill" people, and having focused on freeze and flash points that may be affecting you, LifeMapping also helps you capture the key transitions in your life story—in particular, those you haven't closed the loop on.

4. DEALING WITH UNTIED TRANSITIONS

While it often goes unnoticed or unappreciated, the way you've dealt with the major transitions in your life can have profound implications for your present and future growth.

For some (like a parent launching his or her last child out of the nest), a transition can signal the end of one phase of life. For others (like the person who received an unexpected promotion with triple the responsibilities), it signals a new beginning. Still others (like the spouse who suddenly finds himself or herself a single parent) can find that transitions have instantly forced them to take on unexpected or unwanted roles.

How well you face, process, and move on from major transitions is key to understanding the state of your relationships today. In particular, transitions that remain *untied*—unresolved, not accepted, not adapted to—can be holding you back. In this section of the LifeMapping process, you'll be able to highlight those expected and unexpected transitions and actually discover how God designed us to experience transitions.

Obviously, these first four aspects of LifeMapping all point toward the past. But once you've looked back in a positive way, your next step will be to point your LifeMap toward the future—beginning with a major Y-in-the-road decision.

> The way you've dealt with the major transitions in your life can have profound implications for your present and future growth.

(Stepping Back) . . . to Your Future

5. CHOOSING AUTHENTIC LIVING OVER IMAGE MANAGEMENT

How free are you from what has happened in your past to move toward a positive future? The answer to that question takes each of us to an important Y in the road in our personal lives.

Those who are able to honestly and courageously deal with the past as a learning and shaping tool will take the road that leads to authentic living. That's a way of life that enables us to honestly accept ourselves for who we are—warts, weaknesses, and all.

Yet there's another road we can take. It's a path that starts out wide and inviting but soon turns treacherous. That's the road marked *image management,* and it's a certain way to cycle ourselves back into the past and repeat previous unwanted patterns time and again.

In chapter 9, we'll look at how each of us has a public self and a private self. The degree to which these two aspects are in balance will help determine how fulfilling today is and how solid a foundation we're building for the future. Personally, spiritually, and professionally, avoiding image management and taking the road forward to authentic living is vital to a God-honoring future.

It begins by . . .

6. GAINING A CLEAR PLAN FOR YOUR FUTURE

As I mentioned in chapter 2, having a clear picture of where you'd like to be in your faith, family, and work can add quality, health, and length to your life. Using the storyboarding tool, you can take each important area of your life and lay out goals, dreams, and hopes.

God alone knows the future. However, a clear plan that is open to His leading and prayerfully seeks to make you a more effective servant can help you do more for Christ and others than you may have ever thought possible. "But I've made plans before," you may say, "and they never seem to get off the paper and into my everyday life. Something always seems to come up that keeps me from making the changes I really need to make."

What happens when your clear plan gets muddied by the unexpected twists and turns life often brings? That's when you focus on another LifeMapping tool filled with everyday encouragement to keep pressing forward.

7. PRACTICING LEARNED HOPEFULNESS

The bumps and jolts of real life can sometimes throw you off course, even when you've taken the time to develop a clear plan. However, in this section, you'll learn a powerful way of staying focused on God's best called *learned hopefulness*. You'll see how to avoid feeling helpless when life seems to take a U-turn, and you'll discover how to maintain a "due north" heading toward the hopeful future God has for you.

8. LINING UP MEMORIAL MARKERS FOR LASTING CHANGE

By the time you get to this point in the book, you'll have your past and future LifeMapped, and you'll have applied what you've discovered about image management and learned hopefulness. But while this process can be very motivating, it needs yet another element to make your plans more than just a glorified New Year's resolution.

Here's where the LifeMapping process dips into the Old Testament again and utilizes a concept called *memorial markers* to help you make and maintain positive changes. What's more, these markers can become powerful, tangible reminders of what God has done and is doing in your life.

■

That's an overview of the eight elements of LifeMapping: four reflections of your past and four building blocks to a special future. You may still feel overwhelmed, however, by the task of displaying your whole life story. "I'm fifty-five years old!" you may say. "How in the world can I capture a lifetime of memories and dreams and put them into a format that will make sense?"

How can you do that? The same way Leonardo da Vinci and Walt Disney created masterpieces, the United States Navy created battleships in World War II, and spaceships are being created today! By using storyboarding to create your LifeMap.

PART 2

Stepping Back...

CHAPTER 5

Recognizing Your Strengths, Successes, and "High Hill" People

LifeMapping starts by looking at your past, but as we've seen with that group of people in the church of Ephesus, it's not just about looking at what's gone wrong or off track. In fact, it begins by looking back in a way that might surprise you.

No matter how positive or difficult a background you come from, LifeMapping starts by focusing on your strengths and identifying times of success. What's more, we'll look at how well your successes were celebrated by those closest to you. We'll identify those "high hill" people who lifted you up or whose voice or actions support you in challenges today.

But why start with strengths and successes? After all, for

many of us, a look back simply reveals dark shadows of failure or icy patches of pain, neglect, or regret. When I first started using LifeMapping with individuals and couples, I had a name for the look people gave me when they were hurting—struggling with life or another person or both. I called that look "the stare." I remember one man saying, "Do you really think I'd be in here if I had any strengths?"

Give people an opening, and you'll hear about all that has gone wrong for them and the person or life situation that seems set on defeating them. But that's not where you'll start.

A Guaranteed Test of Success

My first year and very first class at Dallas Seminary, I (John) was as nervous as a cat in a room full of rocking chairs (as my grandfather used to say). While I had struggled through summer-school Greek, this was my first day of regular classes and a full campus. Deep inside, I knew God wanted me in seminary, but I also knew I was being tossed in with the best and the brightest.

I knew the admissions officers at Dallas had turned down nearly three students for every applicant they'd accepted that year. I also knew that among the best and brightest, I'd gotten in on academic probation just days before the summer term started. (I've always wanted to meet the person who dropped out, creating a "let's give the marginal guy a shot" spot for me to attend.)

I showed up early to my first class, and it didn't help when I introduced myself to the person sitting on my right, a pastor's kid and honors graduate from Columbia University.

Looking left made it worse—the person sitting there was a Wheaton College honors student. He'd been to Christian grade school, high school, and college. There I sat, a first-generation Christian, never having even been to Sunday school and now in theology school!

We were waiting for class to start when I caught a first glimpse of a man I'd heard much about. It was Dr. Howard Hendricks, the teacher for this class, a noted Christian educator and one of the first family pastors on the planet. I'm honored to say he would become a mentor and special friend. I walked out of his class on the topic of the Christian home that first day, called my mom from a pay phone, and told her I'd just figured out what I was going to do for the rest of my life. I was going to work with couples and families. But that's getting a bit ahead of the story.

That first day, "Prof" stepped up to the podium right on time. After opening the class in prayer, Dr. Hendricks said in his booming voice, "People, I've got a test for you as we begin this class."

I didn't hear a single groan in the large, amphitheater-style room except my own. *Oh, great*, I thought as I fumbled for my Bible. *Here comes one of those "Name the Old Testament kings" tests that I feared would happen.*

"If you pass this test," Prof said, "I can almost guarantee you'll be a success here at seminary and in your ministry. But if you fail this test, I can almost assure you that you won't be successful in either area."

Let's see, there was Hezekiah, Ahab, Saul, David . . . or was Hezekiah a judge?

"Now take out a 3 × 5 card or piece of paper, and here's the test: Write down your three greatest weaknesses."

Weaknesses? Hold on. Did he really say, "Write down your greatest weaknesses"?

If that's what it took to be a success in seminary and ministry, then my heart soared. I was going to be incredibly successful! I forgot all about the 3 × 5 card and reached for a legal pad instead.

I was just filling up my second sheet of weaknesses when Prof's voice cut in:

"Okay, that was just the warm-up. *Here's the real test.*"

I knew it! I thought, shaking my head. *That guy from Wheaton probably lived in a dorm named after one of those Hebrew kings!*

"Turn your 3 × 5 card over and write down your three greatest strengths."

Strengths? I thought. *Strengths???*

I'd had no trouble listing weaknesses. Yet suddenly I saw that my pen was dead still in my hand. And from my position in the very last row of class, I looked down and noticed that almost everyone else's pen had stopped too.

Why is it so hard for us to see our strengths?

A Second National Pastime

If baseball is still America's national pastime (and it's a toss-up with the NFL), being critical has got to come in a close second. It's not just true of the Washington press corps. As a country, we've become obsessed with cancel culture and blowing up faults.

When was the last time a positive, redeeming story was trending? Why isn't our credit rating more influenced by the years we've paid the mortgage on time rather than on the two payments we missed? Why do studies of both male and female bosses find them pointing out failures four times more often than offering praise?[1]

While there may be some merit in chronicling our failures, I'm convinced that's not where God would have us focus. In fact, it's His desire that we look at a marvelous mirror that can tell us what's *right* with us, not what's wrong.

Mirror, Mirror on the Wall . . .

Did you know that there's a miraculous mirror you can go to anytime that will reflect the brightest and best part of you? It's a mirror not of make-believe, like the talking mirror in *Snow White and the Seven Dwarfs*, but of rock-solid reality. Just open your Bible to 2 Corinthians 3:18 and you'll find the mirror that can reveal your strengths and point you toward the person you'd most like to become.

The apostle Paul put it this way: "But we all, with unveiled faces, looking as in a mirror at the glory of the Lord, are being transformed into the same image from glory to glory, just as from the Lord, the Spirit."

The miraculous mirror Paul described is a picture of all your positive potential and capacity for love. That's because it's a reflection of God's Son and Holy Spirit inside you and the promise of all He can help you to become.

There's actually a double miracle described here. First, you can see the almighty God face-to-face in the mirror (in Jesus, the "image of the invisible God" [Colossians 1:15]). And second, God Himself is committed to transforming— literally, *transfiguring*—you into His glorious image.

Remember Leonardo da Vinci's masterpieces? They started with a sketch of the finished product—beginning with the end in sight. The same thing should be true of you.

It's easy to look at your failures and defeats and, as we'll see in the next element of LifeMapping, your emotional freeze points. But it's necessary to post those challenging parts of our life story as well.

Here at the beginning, it's extremely important that you recall and believe that you also have God-given strengths and high personal value—strengths you can develop today and tomorrow that can increase "glory to glory" to reflect His love all the more. And if you're going through this book to learn how to coach and encourage others, you must start here. In fact, your goal will be—even for someone from a difficult background—to generate dozens of posts under this first element of LifeMapping. Clinically, it's called *flooding*.

> It's extremely important that you recall and believe that you also have God-given strengths and high personal value.

Have you ever been in a room full of fellow employees or ministry workers, and the leader has everyone stop, turn, and say something positive about you, your skills, your work, or your character? Something they see in you that's valuable and important? It does happen, and while it can be uncomfortable, it's usually incredibly meaningful.

It's your job—going through this for yourself first and then for helping others—to start here. Build out on your LifeMap those pictures, stories, and personal strengths and gifts that almighty God has placed inside you. (See 1 Corinthians 12 and Romans 12.)

Once you've identified your strengths, you can more easily look at those times when you've exercised them. It's the exercising of your strengths that leads to your successes.

And finally, we'll look at whether your strengths were celebrated—whether they were ever verbally, tangibly acknowledged by your parents, spouse, or others. These would be words that come from those invaluable "high hill" people I'll say more about shortly. But words of affirmation from such people—their acknowledgment of your personal, God-given strengths and successes—are a key factor in forming the level of acceptance you carry forward in regard to yourself and others each day of your life.

But before we get into chronicling strengths, successes, and times when your strengths were celebrated, let's look at one roadblock that can keep you from ever seeing or remembering any of them. That roadblock can effectively wall off anything positive from your past and ultimately will lead you down a bumpy, dead-end road.

A Potential Roadblock to Posting Even a Single Strength

What's the roadblock I'm talking about? *Legalism.* I agree with my friend Chuck Swindoll that perhaps the greatest danger facing the church today isn't unbridled license but legalism.[2]

In the verses leading up to 2 Corinthians 3:18, Paul pointed out that we must turn from gazing only at rules and look instead at the Giver of life. If the focus of our lives becomes a performance-oriented scorecard handed to us by a modern Pharisee, we'll never see our strengths. That's because solely focusing on rules serves only to condemn us—because we can't keep them! As Romans 3:23 says, "For all have sinned and fall short of the glory of God."

As mentioned, you see this constantly today: People digging into the past and finding a ten-year-old email or lists of tweets or posts that were mean—or worse. People think they're heroes for dragging out the worst and shouting it from the digital rooftops. Even more points for them if they get someone fired or shamed into dropping out of everything. You have to be perfectly in sync with the current religion of wokeness and repression or get ready to be canceled. (That sentence alone makes me worthy of being canceled.)

But there's something that cancel culture can't cancel, and that's courage—the courage to admit that absolutely, we were wrong. Or imperfect. But more than that, the courage to look in that magic mirror we talked about earlier.

When we look at Jesus, His Spirit takes the veil of blindness from our eyes; we accept the forgiveness and newness of life He offers; and we find that our sufficiency is from God (2 Corinthians 3:5, see verses 4-11). Then we discover that in Him, we are free from the condemnation of basing our lives on a set of enslaving rules and daily online drill sergeant inspections. (Jesus knew a lot about that in dealing with his own set of Pharisees and Sadducees.)

Entire lives and cultures are being built on tearing down people, rarely on encouraging them or helping them up. But even if we're imperfect, when we're courageous and resilient enough to get back up when we fall, we'll find we are free to love and serve Him in righteousness from a place of refreshing *acceptance.*

When we have God's love inside us, words still hurt when we're canceled. The mob may still knock us *down.* But never can they knock us *out.* And by God's grace, we already knew we were broken. ("While we were still sinners, Christ died for us" [Romans 5:8].) And even more important, we know Jesus told us something tattoo-worthy in Hebrews 13:5: "For He Himself has said, 'I WILL NEVER DESERT YOU, NOR WILL I EVER ABANDON YOU.'"

You are never alone when Jesus walks with you. Never without worth. Never without a way up and forward.

If all that sounds too spiritual or technical, let me put it another way. *A relationship with Jesus is based on what we can become in Him, not on what we've failed to be in the eyes of others.*

When we become that "new creation" in Christ as God promises (see 2 Corinthians 5:17), we inherit a relationship with someone who forever will look at and develop our strengths—not focus on our weaknesses.

Our teachers may grade us on the curve; our bosses may judge us by how much work we get done; the IRS may force us to account for each penny we earn; and the online mob may drag out that single sentence or long list of emails. But God judges us by a different standard—the Cross. And when we accept Jesus as our Savior and Lord, we've got a secure base on which to build and grow a fulfilling life.

And we need security to do life well. We need to know we're loved. Valuable. Attached. Connected. Cared for. No matter what. And that kind of love *does* exist in a personal relationship with Jesus, who loves us. The very Lord of lords and King of kings values us.

Let's face it, to some extent, we're all damaged goods. But in Jesus, we don't have to focus on what's wrong. Now we're free to focus on our strengths, our spiritual gifts, and the God-given value we have in Him.

So how do we look back at the past and come up with our strengths and successes?

Four (Animal) Faces of Our Strengths

First, let's clarify what we mean by looking for our strengths and examine what qualifies as success. Then we'll look at how you can capture them for use on your LifeMap.

For LifeMapping purposes, our strengths are the God-given abilities, talents, desires, and sensitivities that He has chosen to make a part of our lives. In some cases (like with spiritual gifts), they're things that come with our spiritual birth. In others, they're general tendencies or enjoyable habits or aptitudes we were born with.

Successes, then, are those special times when we've used our strengths to enrich God's Kingdom or the lives of others.

Notice that I've defined *success* not only in terms of personal accomplishment. For example, if we've used our God-given strength of overseeing or directing others to push, shove, or bully them on our way to the top, that's not success, no matter what we've accomplished. Rather, when we use our strengths and talents to empower and benefit others, then we can claim genuine success.

Consider Eric Liddell, the Scottish runner whose life story inspired the wonderful movie *Chariots of Fire*. In one particularly poignant scene, Liddell was debating with his sister whether he should continue running as an Olympic hopeful or head straight to the mission field. She seemed crestfallen when he announced his intention to put off missions temporarily for the chance at a medal. But instead of shaming or arguing with her, he comforted her with the words "Jenny, Jenny, you've got to understand. I believe that God made me for a purpose. For China. But He also made me fast. And when I run, I feel His pleasure."[3]

That's one way to look at our strengths. In this case, God had given Liddell a special ability to run. And in exercising that talent, he felt God's approval. The use of that talent not only blessed him, but it also provided a platform from which to encourage many others.

I'm not saying that all strengths are physical talents like running, mountain biking, or skating. Nor do our strengths have to win us a gold medal or become the basis of an Academy Award–winning movie. Instead, more often, God gives us everyday strengths that fall into one of four areas. See if you can recognize some of your strengths in one, two, or even all four of the following areas.

An Outstanding Tool for Helping See Our Strengths: The Connect Assessment

Years ago, I came up with an animal personality model based on a four-factor assessment, where people could see their strengths. It uses lions, otters, golden retrievers, and beavers. It's all fleshed out in the book I wrote with my friend of friends, Gary Smalley, called *The Two Sides of Love*. Today, Kari and I train life coaches to be StrongFamilies Strengths

Coaches based on the LOGB model. (Go to ICCIcoaching .com for more about becoming a Strengths Coach.) At the heart of our training, thanks to the incredible work by Dr. Dewey Wilson at StrongMarriages.com, there's an online version of this assessment.

One of the first things we have people do to understand their strengths, and that we encourage you to do now, is take the time to go online and take the free short form of the Connect Assessment (StrongFamilies.com/LOGB).

The website will take you to an assessment that gives you a graph full of important information about who you are. It's an incredibly powerful way to see the strengths God has placed inside you. (There is an opportunity to upgrade to a fourteen-page paid assessment that we use to flood people with their strengths, but the free graph is a great starting point and all you need to make your LifeMap.)

What you'll see is whether you're a lion, otter, golden retriever, or beaver personality. If you're a lion, words and phrases that describe you are *takes charge, determined, assertive, firm, purposeful, decision maker*, and *adventurous*.

If you're an otter, you'll see words like *visionary, energetic, verbal, avoids details, fun-loving*, and *group-oriented*.

If you're a golden retriever, you'll see words like *loyal, avoids conflict, patient, sympathetic, adaptable, nurturing*, and *good listener*.

And if you're a beaver, you'll see words like *deliberate, controlled, practical, factual, persistent, scheduled*, and *discerning*.

The goal here is to help you understand that there really is a whole list of positive things God has placed inside you—traits, gifts, strengths, abilities, and insights that He has used and can still use in your life story. But we tend to see these strengths discounted or disappear when we're struggling or lost or feel as if we've failed.

To some degree, we all have verbal strengths like an otter personality. As you think back on your past, perhaps you can identify some special verbal skills God has given you to encourage others. You may sing in the church choir, use your voice to sell insurance that protects people who have suffered from catastrophes, or stand up and challenge a teacher who is tearing down truth. Perhaps you're good at writing notes of encouragement or speaking out in public to protect biblical values or advocate for the unborn.

Using your Connect Assessment, thinking about how God has gifted you, and asking others who care about you to add to your list are powerful ways to come up with words and phrases—even a story captured on a post—that highlight those verbal strengths you have developed or have used to help others. These are important things to put on your LifeMap.

For others of us, our God-given strengths are seen in the ability we have to take things apart and see key ways to refine processes, like a hardworking beaver. Perhaps you're a high school coach who has drawn up successful plays since you were a child on the sandlots. You may be an accomplished web designer or data processor. Or you might be a church business administrator who, after twenty years of keeping the Navy in line, now keeps the church records shipshape.

All those orderly traits can reflect a special ability to

make the lives of others better and less cluttered. As with any strength, this one can sometimes be pushed too far and become a weakness (like the organized person who becomes enslaved to an unbendable schedule). If you get personal satisfaction, however, and "feel God's pleasure" in a job well organized and well planned, all that can be captured and posted on your LifeMap.

Many of us carry sensing strengths that are just what they sound like: that special ability to feel the hurts of others—to perceive what that person in front of you is really like and to communicate warmth and encouragement to meet the person's need. Often, these are our golden retriever friends.

An example of this skill showed up in a study of excellent nurses. They discovered that patients who interacted regularly with nurses who were "warm, sensitive, and likable" took less medicine for pain and discomfort! In other words, by sensing and empathizing with their patients' pain, these nurses actually helped relieve the hurt and aches.[4]

I'm not suggesting that those with sensing strengths are human aspirin bottles, but that's one way to look at their God-given skills. Have you ever been around someone who seemed to make you feel better just by listening to you? Are you that type of person? Have you had others comment that you're a loyal or sensitive friend? Do you get particular pleasure out of simply "being there" for a friend who is working through a problem—even if you don't get up-front credit for doing so?

Again, those are things you'll want to list and post on your LifeMap under strengths.

And so, too, are those strengths that often show up in

lions. Taking on a challenge brings you fulfillment and makes you feel alive—especially if you have gotten to direct something or a group of people toward a purposeful conclusion or past a big obstacle. You find it particularly gratifying when someone has said, "You can't do that!" and yet you got it done.

It may have been anything from producing the second-grade play to leading a recon platoon in combat to running for public office to making sure things work smoothly in your home. But the common denominator is that from your position as point person, you were leading the parade, taking on a challenge, and enjoying it.

Now that you have a better idea of what's meant by strengths, you're ready to begin capturing them on your LifeMap. And take a special note here: We encourage our LifeMapping coaches to come up with twenty to thirty subber cards that capture someone's strengths. Yes, that's a lot, but we hear so little today about who we are positively and how we've been gifted with strengths. I'll go back to that test Dr. Hendricks gave us on the first day of seminary class. Seeing our strengths is a powerful way to get us moving toward helping others, tackling life, and breaking free from feeling we *have* nothing or *are* nothing.

Storyboarding Your Strengths and Successes

It's time to pull out your LifeMap and begin putting cards under the topper labeled Strengths, Successes, and "High Hill" People. And to show you how that's done, let's go back to my LifeMap as an illustration of what you can do with your own.

You'll see in mine a topper and a line of subbers that have all eight of the LifeMapping elements. Start with the first. Each strength or success or supportive "high hill" person you'll post will go under that first topper card.

As I thought back on the strengths and successes in my life story, I posted seven things from the list I came up with myself and with the help of others. (Again, it's fine to have dozens of subbers here, and that's a goal we shoot for with our coaches. But for the sake of space, I'll put just a few subbers under each main LifeMapping element throughout the book.)

The first subber I posted was an experience that pointed out a strength I'd been given, but in a difficult way. You'll see that first post is "Making up for math with letters." Let me tell you the story behind that.

I remember sitting in a doctoral class one day where we were studying how to construct, conduct, and interpret various types of tests. Every student had to take numerous kinds of tests, including an IQ test.

With each assessment we took as a class, our professor would randomly pick someone and go over his or her assessment as the class example.

I had taken an IQ test before, but I had never actually seen the results, so I didn't mind when the professor chose me as the IQ test example. At first, that is.

"Now, John," the professor said, looking over my results. "This shows that you scored extremely high in the verbal and writing portions of the test."

I humbly nodded and tried not to act too proud in front of the other, less gifted students.

Then my bubble burst. The professor went on: "But I

need to ask you, did you go through a very difficult birth experience, or were you ever held underwater for a long period of time?"

"What?" I stammered, not understanding where his question was coming from. "No, sir," I managed to get out. "I can't say either thing has happened to me. Why?"

"Well," he said, gazing intently at my test scores, "you're very high in the verbal and writing section—but you're four points away from brain damage when it comes to the mathematical and spatial orientation sections!"

Brain damage?

For each semester thereafter, you can guess how many jokes I endured from my classmates. While that particular day was humiliating, I realized, upon reflection, what God had done. He had helped compensate for my poor math and spatial skills with words!

I would need every bit of those verbal skills to talk my way through the one and only math class I took in college. It was a course in elementary sets. (Remember sets and subsets?) As simple as that class was, I would have flunked if the teacher hadn't let me *write* and use my words in an extra-credit paper to pull out a passing grade.

God had helped compensate for my poor math and spatial skills with words!

So verbal strengths went on my LifeMap. And if you look closer, you'll also see that I've listed some sensing strengths like "Team Player" and "Encourager." Those are reflections of the enjoyment I get in encouraging and serving others.

"Decade" Your Life Story and Make as Long a List as You Can of Successes

In addition to working to capture your strengths, it's also time to add posts that reflect the application of those strengths. In other words, what have you done in your life story that was a success?

For example, I've been blessed with a wonderful wife and two daughters (and now two great sons-in-law and grandchildren). I've worked hard at being a good husband and father. Also, by using my writing skills, God has allowed me to finish some books and gain a few awards along the way ("Work awards" on the LifeMap) that have highlighted those skills.

I state these not to pat myself on the back but to do what God repeatedly asked us to do—remember His faithfulness in giving us our strengths, and also be thankful for successes when we've put our strengths to use. Whether your successes were finishing high school or basic training, volunteering at the hospital, or manning a space station, put them in your LifeMap.

You might want to start at the decade level to help draw out the successes God has given you. In other words, think of "In my teens . . ." or "In my twenties . . ." or "In my thirties . . ." and keep going. It's a great way to go back through your life story and see how, time after time, the Lord has helped you accomplish something that goes under this Success heading.

And let me address here what can and does happen to some.

If you can't think of even one strength you have, take that objective Connect Assessment test to get past the roadblock or legalism that keeps you from saying anything positive to or about yourself. And the same is true in terms of successes. If you can't think of a single success you've had, it's most often because of the failures you've experienced. It's like having a wayward child and feeling you're a failure at parenting, even if your other children didn't choose that path. Now is not the time to list all those hurts and roadblocks that can stop you from "remembering from where you've fallen." Go through each decade. Look for strengths. Ask God to bring to mind (and thank Him for!) your successes as well.

And now note that phrase we've shared several times already: "high hill" people. This is also the place in your LifeMap to list those "high hill" people who saw and stood beside you and *celebrated* who you are or what you accomplished. Let's take a closer look.

Opening Our Eyes to See and Be Grateful for "High Hill" People

What in the world is a "high hill" person? The concept is based on a study by Dr. Dennis Proffitt at the University of Virginia. His subject was visual perception. He and his colleagues would get someone who was alone to stand and look up at a high hill on the UVA campus. Then they'd put a heavy backpack on that person and have him or her judge how high the hill was and how hard it would be to climb.

But they did something else in the study as well. They also recruited pairs who came by—two friends or perhaps a dating couple. Again the hill was pointed out, but the two people were told they would be climbing the hill together.

In each case, those who were alone perceived the high hill as even higher, steeper, and harder to climb than it actually was. But those people who had someone with a hand on their shoulder, ready to climb the hill with them, saw the challenge before them shrink. The hill became, in their perception, less steep and less difficult to climb.

Seriously? Just someone putting a hand on your shoulder and saying they're going to climb that hill with you has such an impact on your perception? Well, ask soldiers who have gone into battle alongside a friend versus those who have had to go it alone. Or you can do what other researchers did to test Proffitt's findings at UVA.

A follow-up study was done at the University of Plymouth in England. Only this time, when they had people stand alone and look up at a high hill, they asked them to just *think about* a person in their life standing there with them, with a hand on their shoulder, and then climbing that high hill with them.

Again, those people who were alone, without a "high hill" person's mental picture with them, saw the challenges before them as higher, steeper, harder. Yet those with even just the thought of someone committed to going up the hill with them experienced more courage to tackle the climb. And the hill shrank.[5]

That's what we're looking for in your life story. Maybe someone like my mother. She had rheumatoid arthritis and could never have actually climbed that high hill with me. But when I think about my life story, I know she had her hand on my shoulder all my life. Through every challenge, she was there. And today, though she's now in heaven, just the memory of her being there for my brothers and me still shrinks the hills I face.

And no, "high hill" people don't have to be perfect. Consider the story of Roger.

Roger and I went to grade school and high school together. I felt I knew him well, but there was something about him that confused me. He always seemed so confident and quick to encourage others. He has since gone on to do well in his vocation, and he married and has a wonderful, loving family. Yet as I watched him growing up, I knew he came from a very troubled household. It wasn't the kind of environment you'd think would cause him to turn out so well.

For example, I remember being at his house when his dad would stumble in drunk and we kids would be ordered outside by his mom. I also recall that at age fifteen, on the day before a major game we were to play, Roger was called out of practice and informed that his father had died.

I'd seen firsthand the effects of an alcoholic father (my own), and I had always been impressed by the way Roger had coped and grown through it. But it wasn't until recently, when I brought this up to him, that he told me something that floored me.

I had congratulated him on beating the odds and building a strong family despite having such a tough background. He responded, "But, John, you don't realize something. It's true my dad drank. Sometimes way too much. And when he died, it really hurt. But I had something to hang on to.

"You wouldn't know it," he continued, "but every single day of my life that I can remember, my father would come into my room before bedtime. And every night, he'd tell me how proud he was of me for what I'd done that day in school or sports. I must have heard hundreds of times how special I was to him and how much he loved me. Even after those nights when he'd been drinking, when he would sober up, he'd ask me to forgive him. And he always told me I had a wonderful future ahead of me—one without alcohol."

While it didn't show to those of us outside his family, Roger had a hidden source of inner strength given to him by his imperfect but loving father. In those bedtime visits, he heard his strengths celebrated repeatedly by an adoring dad. And that's what has helped in filling up his need for acceptance over the years.

If There Really Were No "High Hill" People . . .

We've looked at God-given strengths and successes. We've also seen that when those strengths are celebrated by a "high hill" person, it can help us deal with challenges and shrink the obstacles we face. Unfortunately, some of us came from homes where we never heard our strengths celebrated. As a result, the dipstick isn't touching oil when it comes to feeling accepted and acceptable and free to chart a positive course for the future.

Look at sixteen-year-old Darren, for example. His father was an angry alcoholic who had left him and his mother and sister six years before. But now that Darren was the captain of his small-town basketball team, his father wanted to use him for bragging rights with his drinking buddies.

Darren remembers the last time he saw his father. His dad was standing inside a raunchy saloon, demanding that Darren come in and have a drink with him to celebrate the big game. But mindful of a mother who had warned him to never step inside a bar, Darren told his father, "If you want to talk to me, sober up and come to one of my games."

As Darren walked away, the old man screamed at him, "Don't walk away from me! You're worthless! You're nothing but scum! You'll never amount to anything!"

That was hardly a celebration of Darren's strengths. And it was particularly hard to swallow when his dad died years later, and those scorching words were the last Darren would ever hear from him.

Perhaps you came from a home where your strengths were never mentioned, never appreciated, never celebrated. If so, don't be surprised if you can't think of a single thing to put on cards in this column—at least until you deal with the next element of LifeMapping, emotional freeze points. As you'll see in the next chapter, you can begin to thaw out from those difficult seasons of life and find God's strength to go on.

Overcoming Evil with Good

We've seen that God invites us to look into His mirror and see all the good things we can become in His Son. What's more, we've seen that God has gifted each of us with valuable strengths, whether they are verbal, analytical, sensing, or directing.

For all of us, recognizing and building on our strengths is an important place to begin, not only in the LifeMapping process but in building a fulfilling life as well.

Focusing on your strengths—and on the application of those strengths, which produces your successes—will often reduce or eliminate your weaknesses. You get so focused on the positive goal in front of you (helping, serving, leading, encouraging) that you cut down on the time, energy, and desire to maintain the negative. And when your strengths get celebrated, you're in the best place to turn around and do the same for others.

A Reminder to Build and Bless the Strengths of Others

We need to be people who recognize and thank God for the strengths He's given us. And we also need to point out the strengths in others' lives.

You may be a parent who can celebrate your child's strengths. You may be a neighbor who offers encouragement across a fence. You may be a coach who builds a positive legacy like basketball legend John Wooden at UCLA. You may be a pastor who can change lives by acknowledging and affirming parishioners' strengths.

Or maybe you're just an everyday person with an everyday job who can make a life-changing difference by pointing out others' gifts and abilities. Sister Helen Mrosla was such a person.

She remembers her first teaching experience. There were thirty-four third-graders in her class in Morris, Minnesota, all of them filled with youthful bounce.

Sister Mrosla vividly recalls one young man named Mark who talked incessantly. He was handsome, and in every way except that constant chattering, he was well-behaved. Finally, in total frustration one afternoon, Sister Mrosla issued an ultimatum she instantly wished she'd left unsaid: "If you open your mouth one more time, Mark, I'm going to tape it closed!"

As you can imagine, it wasn't two minutes later before another student shouted out, "Mark's talking! Mark's talking!"

Since the punishment had been stated in front of the class, Sister Mrosla was stuck. So, too, were Mark's lips when she very purposefully (and with the room falling into a deep hush) proceeded to Mark's desk, tore off two pieces of tape, and made a big X over his mouth. Then she returned to her desk.

As she glanced at Mark to see how he was doing, he winked at her, and soon she was chuckling and then laughing out loud. The entire class cheered as she walked back to Mark's desk and removed the tape. His first words after the tape came off were "Thank you for correcting me, Sister."

Several years passed, and Mark found himself in Sister Mrosla's class again. Now it was junior high, and she had moved on to teaching math. At one point, she could sense that it was the time of year when students were getting on each other's nerves. The frustration increased as they had tried and failed to understand a difficult concept all week, and friction seemed to permeate the room.

"Take out two sheets of paper," she told the class at the end of that trying week, "and write down the names of each student in the room on those two sheets of paper, leaving a space between each name. Now I want you to think of the nicest thing you can say about each of your classmates, and write that down beneath their name."

Sister Mrosla had the class take the rest of the period to finish the assignment, and that weekend, she listed each child's name on a separate sheet of paper, then compiled everything positive that everyone else had said about that individual under the name. On Monday, she gave each child his or her list. And while everyone seemed pleased, no one ever mentioned those papers in class again.

Years passed, and one day Sister Mrosla was returning from a vacation. Her parents met her at the airport. As they were driving home, her father cleared his throat and said, "Mark Eklund's family called last night. You know, he was in your class."

"Really?" she said. "I haven't heard from them in several years. I wonder how Mark is."

Her father responded quietly, "Mark was killed in Vietnam. The funeral is tomorrow, and his parents would like it if you could attend."

The church was packed, and the service was a tribute to a fallen hero. But afterward, something totally unexpected happened. Mark's mother and father came up to Sister Mrosla and said, "We want to show you something." Opening his wallet, the father pulled out a wad of papers.

"They found this on Mark when he was killed," he said. "We thought you might recognize it."

He carefully revealed two worn pieces of notebook paper that had obviously been taped, folded, and refolded many times. The papers were the ones on which Sister Mrosla had listed all the good things Mark's classmates had said about him that day in junior high school.

"Thank you so much for doing that," Mark's mother said. "As you can see, Mark treasured it."[6]

When you point out another person's strengths, you may be creating a memory he or she carries for a lifetime— or into the next. You might do something as simple as picking up the phone and making double sure your grown children know they're special and deeply loved, possessing strengths you can celebrate. It may involve something as easy as turning off the television and sitting beside your son

When you point out another person's strengths, you may be creating a memory he or she carries for a lifetime—or into the next. who is such a good reader, making sure he knows you appreciate that gift. Or it might be something as minor as showing up at a practice—not even a game—and pointing out your daughter's persistence in her team sport.

We've looked at the first element of LifeMapping—recognizing your strengths, successes, and those "high hill" people who have taken the time to encourage you and to put their hand on your shoulder and climb challenges with you. If this first element can get you off to a positive start on the rest of your life, the second—emotional freeze points—can slow your growth down to a crawl unless you learn how to recognize and deal with them.

Digging Deeper

1. First Corinthians 12:4-7 and Ephesians 2:10 describe how each of us has been given spiritual strengths (gifts) and work to do. Read these passages and consider the following questions:

   a. Who provided these abilities?

   b. To whom have they been given, and why?

2. Think of someone you know whom you consider to be gifted. How does he or she use that gift? Do you know someone who has a gift that he or she doesn't use? Why do you think that is? How does that affect that person or the people around him or her?

3. If you haven't already done so, list some of your strengths, successes, and "high hill" people on 3 × 5 subber cards. Be as honest and objective as you can. Can you tie these strengths into some of your successes? (Refer to Dr. Trent's definition of *successes* on page 62.)

CHAPTER 6

Emotional Freeze Points

Novelist Willa Cather wrote, "Most of the basic material a writer works with is acquired before the age of fifteen."[1] And if you think about it, that's often true. Most of Mark Twain's adventure stories, like *The Adventures of Tom Sawyer* and *The Adventures of Huckleberry Finn*, were inspired by his own boyhood experiences. Much of Harper Lee's novel *To Kill a Mockingbird* was based on reflections of her days before age fifteen. And on the darker side, Stephen King has said that childhood fears and traumas greatly influenced his horror writings.

Those who write stories—or live them—are all surrounded and shaped by their early memories. One author, Morris Massey, has built an entire system of values formation around this tenet: You are who you were when you were ten years old. When it comes to the past, whether key events happened when we were ten, fifteen, or pushing fifty, we can be affected by memories.

Unfortunately, some of us are also *controlled* by them.

As you seek to map out your life, you need to look back honestly and see if there were any dark, treacherous, "black ice" patches in your past—cold seasons of hurt, especially if they came before age fifteen—that can cause you to skid off the road of Christlikeness and plow right into an emotional freeze point.

In the previous chapter, we focused on our strengths by looking back. In this chapter, we need to look at those slippery spots in your LifeMap that may have taken you into the ditches. If you can face the hurt and put such difficult times in context, you're in the best position to move past those often-gripping memories and on toward your high calling in Jesus.

Our look at emotional freeze points will begin with a case sudy, followed by a definition, and then we'll consider several ways to understand and begin to overcome those challenging times and get back on the high road. But one thing we can't do is ignore those icy patches. That's something Jamie tried, and she carries the scar to prove it.

A View of Jamie's LifeMap

We met Jamie at a conference where we spoke about memorial markers, the eighth element of LifeMapping. The seminar had been recommended to her by her counselor, who felt she needed to hear its message. As Jamie learned about

LifeMapping and memorial markers, and then reflected on what she had been learning in counseling, two things fell into place for her. See if you can find them in this brief, edited excerpt of her LifeMap.

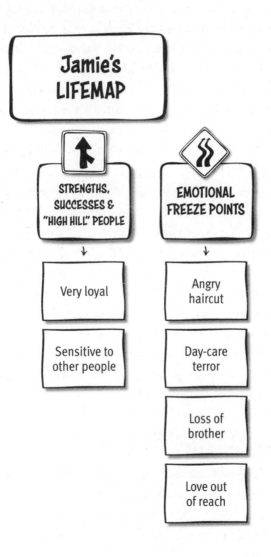

Strengths, Successes, and Acceptance Levels

Jamie's life story was one of strengths in the sensing area that were never recognized or celebrated, and of her hand being slapped away by everyone she reached out to love. She had a huge hole in her life when it came to experiencing any attachment with a significant person.

One of her earliest memories was of playing with scissors and cutting off several snippets of a baby doll's hair. She remembers her mother thundering at her about what a "horrible" child she was to "destroy" such an expensive toy before proceeding to slam her into a chair and cut off her hair in huge clumps so she could "see what it feels like" (as if a doll could really feel).

Regular traumatic trials like that were replicated in a day care setting that was also a living nightmare. While most day care settings are warm and supportive, Jamie was placed in an overcrowded room with an overworked, uncaring staff. Being separated from her mother brought tears to her eyes and contempt from busy teachers. She was labeled a crybaby and pushed aside until she could "grow up."

Can you see the faulty path that began to develop in Jamie's life story? She started with God-given skills of sensing, relating, and desiring to help and encourage others. She was a young girl with a deep need for love and an equally deep longing to love others. Yet it seemed that each turn of life took her toward a painful dead end.

Her father had left the home when Jamie was young, and he never looked back. Her mother was too busy and too preoccupied with work and other children to bother with her. Her older brother, whom she adored, would stand up for her at home and at school. But he also lay upstairs in his room for months, finally dying of Hodgkin's disease when she was still in grade school.

Years passed and Jamie grew up, but even the men she dated treated her terribly. It was always the same story—her trying to please them in vain attempts to receive their love, and them taking advantage of and finally rejecting her instead.

In fact, as Dr. Stephen Madosky says, it is simply too difficult for people to grow up believing they are not loved by their primary caregivers, their parents. If they grow up with abuse instead of love, *then that's what love looks like* to them.

That mirrored the way Jamie would date abusive men. She finally broke up with one man who used and abused her for two years. Eventually, Jamie came to a conclusion as dark as the winter clouds: If all roads in her life led to pain, what use was it to keep trying? That's when she picked up a knife and slid it across her wrist.

She wasn't serious about killing herself, though. It was a gesture of frustration and a cry for help. But the pain and small cut acted like a wake-up call that shocked her into realizing how depressed she'd become, and it pushed her into a counselor's office. In the days and weeks that followed, her supportive Christian counselor became both her coach and her friend.

Jamie's therapist had her go through LifeMapping to capture her strengths, which she struggles with, and lay out those seasons of hurt she experienced as well. But when Jamie got to this part of the LifeMapping process, she almost quit.

She had only come up with two cards in the strengths column, and she had far more than twenty that described freeze points. But then something happened, just by looking at those topper cards she still had to fill out. She had lived with the feeling that her entire life was under that freeze point topper. Looking at all that blank space to the right of her freeze points, however, convinced her that her life story didn't have to *end* in a freeze point.

"I still have a small scar on my hand and wrist," she wrote. "It's not real noticeable, but it's there. But God is healing my wounds. In fact, now every time I look at that scar, it has become a memorial marker of God's love to me, saying, 'Jamie, I also carry scars. I know and have also felt sorrow and pain like you. You don't have to hurt yourself again.'"

Whether you've got one card or twenty under the freeze point topper on your LifeMap, writing them down is one way to begin removing them from your everyday memory. As to how you do that, let's gain a clear definition of what I mean by *freeze point* and how you can begin to break free.

What Exactly Is an Emotional Freeze Point?

An emotional freeze point is a season of time over which unexamined and unprocessed layers of hurt are laid down, restricting or blocking personal and spiritual growth.

A freeze point is most likely to occur when you've never processed a trial, when you've left it unexamined.

You'll notice several important distinctions in the definition. First, freeze points are linked with a length of time. In the next element of LifeMapping, we'll look at those things that *instantaneously* break upon us (flash points) and can have good or bad results. But freeze points are more like the creeping of winter on a northern lake. First, the tilt of the earth's axis positions a hemisphere away from the sun, and the days become shorter. Then the frost on the water begins to sheet. And finally, layers of cold rain and snow add inches to what can become an icy, immovable cover.

Second, not all seasons of hurt cause a freeze point. A freeze point is most likely to occur when you've never processed a trial, when you've left it unexamined. If you've never been willing to talk about past hurts with the Lord, a pastor, or a close friend, then just like that frozen lake, you're adding layers of emotional ice with the passage of time. But if you can honestly take what has happened and turn it toward the warming light of God's love, you can see even difficult times draw you closer to Him.

Consider Joe, for example. On the next page is a picture of his LifeMap's freeze points; the events listed there should have left him with three feet of ice, yet they didn't.

If anyone could have been a model for emotional freeze points, it had to be Joe—that is, Joseph in the Old Testament. He got the multicolored robe from his father, and his brothers got so angry that they tricked him, tied him up, and threw him in a pit in order to kill him. Only by God's grace and an older brother's conscience was Joseph allowed to live instead of becoming food for the wolves.

But if being hated and rejected by his brothers didn't create a freeze point, what happened next should have. He was sold into slavery. Even though he drew a cushy assignment in the house of Potiphar, a wealthy aristocrat, that man's adulterous wife repeatedly tried to get Joseph to sleep with her. In a true instance of sexual harassment, Joseph ran from her lust and was rewarded by being framed and thrown into prison!

Being behind bars would cause a freeze point in almost anyone's life, but here again, Joseph decided to keep moving forward, not freeze inside. He soon worked hard enough to

Joe's
LIFEMAP

EMOTIONAL
FREEZE POINTS

Hated by
his brothers

Thrown into
a pit to die

Sold into
slavery

Sent to prison
in a frame-up

Ignored by friend
who could have
helped him

become the manager of the entire prison, and he was even able to offer help to two friends.

Joseph endured poor family relationships, being plucked out of a well and sold into slavery, suffering the consequences of being unjustly accused of attempted rape after weeks of harassment, and finally being tossed into prison. Those four seasons of pain should have provided enough ice for an Alaskan ice-fishing tournament! And there was more to come.

After turning to God to interpret a dream for a prison friend and seeing that man released, Joseph was promised help and a hearing to clear him of wrongdoing. But what he got instead was a fifth instance in which a protracted, painful experience could have produced a freeze point. In this case, it was a "friend" who forgot to put in a good word for him and left Joseph to toil in prison for many more months.

If you'd been betrayed that often and that dramatically by family, employers, and friends, don't you think you'd be suffering from a freeze point by now? But Joseph had a secret weapon that worked better than electric socks in a cold Chicago winter. He had a God who allowed him to carry his own weather inside him—someone whose love was so warm, whose character was so bright, that even cold nights in a dark prison cell couldn't keep spring from erupting in Joseph's commitment and spirit.

Joseph did many things right. In fact, he responded in ways that many of us might not. What *didn't happen* in Joseph's life that normally occurs when we experience a season of pain and leave it unexamined and unprocessed? Actually, there were three things he *didn't* do. Throughout the rest of the chapter, we'll examine those three things that make all the difference between staying warm and free or being frozen solid emotionally.

The Marks of an Emotional Freeze Point

Read carefully in the next few pages about the characteristics of a freeze point. Take particular note if you find yourself living as if they're part of your story but you can't think of anything obvious that constituted a freeze point. If that's the case, it's time to go back through your personal history and, this time, look for the *less* obvious.

Perhaps you grew up in a home where Mom and Dad stayed together. You were never beaten. No one forced you to clean chimneys or denied you permission to go to the king's ball (or play sports or join the band). It may even have been a home where you were taken to church on Sundays and celebrated Christmas at a midnight candlelight service. But outward looks can be deceiving.

Take a closer look. Perhaps you came from a home where image was put above true intent and actions. (We'll devote an entire chapter to talk about homes that practice image management in the fifth element of LifeMapping.) Or you may have come from a home that looked harmless but conveyed one of the most damaging messages of all, the double message that says, "I'm always here . . . but you can never come to me."

That's the kind of home where a father is simply a shadow that slips in and out, or a mother is far too busy with "important" or "grown-up" things to spend time with the children. Like looking at a broken candy machine, the kids can see what they want but are never able to get to it.

If you felt like an emotional orphan in your home, even though your parents stayed together, it's time to face the truth. The lack of positives from an unattached parent can be just as damaging as the presence of obvious negatives (like yelling, fighting, or divorce).

So if you search your heart (and perhaps even ask your spouse or a close friend) and find that you exhibit all the following characteristics, you're almost certainly suffering the aftereffects of an emotional freeze point.

Freeze points cause us to make pessimism a lifestyle choice.

A lifestyle of pessimism is a common indicator of one or more freeze points. I'm not talking about being a critical thinker or one who thinks things through from all sides. Pessimism is more than that. It's a deep-seated layer of emotional ice that refuses to see hope on the horizon.

It's like the man who went to a psychiatrist because he was depressed. "What's the matter?" the doctor asked.

"Two months ago, my cousin died and left me $100,000," the man said. "Then last month, a great-aunt passed away and left me $500,000."

"Then why are you depressed?"

"This month . . . nothing!"

That's what pessimism does to us. It's not a character trait of cautiousness but an unattractive callus that develops over our ability to have faith and hope. And this pessimism growing out of seasons of hurt can literally be killing us.

People have often dismissed optimism as silliness or even mental illness. Consider these examples:

Optimism is a mania for maintaining that all is well when things are going badly.
VOLTAIRE, 1759

The place where optimism most flourishes is a
lunatic asylum.

HAVELOCK ELLIS, 1923

Pessimism is only the name that men of weak nerves
give to wisdom.

BERNARD DE VOTO, 1935[2]

But clinical research and biblical truth show they're wrong. True optimism is formed when we see life as having meaning; when our life story has a purpose; when we see our LifeMap heading ultimately in a positive direction, even in the midst of trials.

Furthermore, genuine optimism always moves people to positive action. It moved Joseph to action, not apathy, when he worked his way to the top in Potiphar's household and in prison. And it was surely protecting his health as well.

While no Egyptian tablets have yet been unearthed from Joseph's day showing the positive medical effects of being optimistic, we can be sure he benefited from a biblically positive attitude. Put another way, this is the first thing Joseph didn't do: He didn't let self-pity take away his optimistic outlook. Today we have multiple studies linking health and optimism, and one of the best came from the Harvard Study of Adult Development headed most recently by Dr. George E. Vaillant at the Harvard Medical School.

The study began with a group of physically and mentally healthy members of the Harvard classes of 1942 through 1944. In all, 268 young men were included. The study has continued unabated until today and has provided invaluable insights into those men's lives and health. (In fact, only ten men withdrew from the study during college, and two more since graduation.)

Each year, the men have voluntarily taken health and psychological tests to gather data across their life span. Even into their seventies, eighties, and beyond, one finding stands out loud and clear: Overall, those men who were classified as optimists at age twenty-five were far healthier than those who viewed life and its circumstances pessimistically. In other words, optimism early in life is associated with good health later in life.[3]

And that's not just a finding reserved for Harvard students. In a major study done at the University of Michigan on those in the workplace, researchers found that the more optimistic people were, the fewer sick days they reported and the fewer times they reported being ill at all.[4] As an example, researchers from the University of Michigan and Harvard University found that optimism—an expectation that good things will happen—among people aged fifty and older significantly reduced their risk of heart failure. Compared to the least optimistic people in the study, the most optimistic people had a 73 percent reduced risk of heart failure over the follow-up period.[5] Even certain cancer patients have been shown to live longer and go into remission more often and for longer periods if they have a more optimistic view of their circumstances and future.[6]

But why?

A doctor might chalk it up to the effects of immuno-competence, specifically T4 (helper) cells and T8 (suppresser) cells. The *helper* and *suppresser* labels reflect the roles those cells play in turning on and off the body's fight against infections. A high ratio (where helper cells outnumber suppresser cells) means a robust, on-the-attack immune system. A low ratio means a weak immune system, with fewer helper cells and relatively more suppresser cells.[7]

As you might have guessed by now, even the blood work done on optimists and pessimists shows a difference in their immunocompetence. Optimists tend to have higher levels of helper cells, and pessimists tend to have more suppresser cells—just as Vaillant's study and many others would suggest.

But clinical studies are only part of the picture. If you're suffering from an emotional freeze point, you're *probably* putting your physical health at risk. But you're *certainly* putting your relational health at risk.

WHEN PAIN AND PESSIMISM WALK DOWN THE AISLE

Dr. John Gottman at the University of Washington studied more than three thousand married couples over two decades. What he discovered about how wives and husbands relate to each other is so remarkable that he could predict, with 94 percent accuracy, which marriages would succeed and which would fail![8]

In his landmark research, he found that for a marriage to last, there must be at least five positive interactions for every negative one between partners. And what happens when one person has a trapped layer of emotional hurt that produces a critical, negative attitude? He calls it a cycle of negativity that can cave in on a couple and end their marriage.

That's when the four relationship killers he isolated—criticism, contempt, defensiveness, and rigidity—form a deepening spiral that leads to more criticism, greater contempt, increasing defensiveness, and stone-wall rigidity.

Who displays such attitudes? In his studies, it was often people who come into marriage with a history of emotional hurt (i.e., periods when there were freeze points) and who have become critical pessimists in their marriages. And such people are not found only in secular circles. They're also scattered throughout the church.

COMING HOME WITH A HUG

One day, several years ago, my wife, Cindy, came home from a Bible study group. Although we're an affectionate couple anyway, this day she threw her arms around me the moment she saw me, and for the longest time she refused to let go.

"What have you been studying at your Bible study?" I asked. "Song of Solomon? If this is the homework, why don't you all meet twice a week!"

She assured me they hadn't been studying the romantic Song of Solomon. "We've been studying what the Scriptures say about a 'critical spirit.' And the reason I hugged you was that out of the five women in my group, I'm the only one who doesn't live with a critical husband."

Granted, her group was overloaded with women living with pessimists, but many men and women face that challenge. And as it says in the book of Proverbs, "It is better to live on a corner of the roof, than in a house shared with a contentious woman [or man]" (Proverbs 25:24).

"But I'm not a critical pessimist!" you might say. Well, to help you get a better idea of whether you are or aren't, ask yourself if you've said or thought anything like these statements in the past six months of your marriage:

- "I feel it's important to determine whose fault it is when there's an argument."
- "He (she) always comes at things from his (her) side only."

- "I don't censor my complaints when I'm angry. I just let it rip."
- "Sure, I'm negative at times, but that gets things off my chest."
- "I don't start an argument unless I know I'm right."
- "I don't have to take this kind of treatment from anybody."
- "We've tried and tried to change. Nothing works."
- "This is just one more area of my life where another person has killed my dreams."

Studies of pessimists reveal that they make a great number of critical comments—criticizing both themselves and those with whom they live. And often without realizing it, they do so at high cost to both their personal and their marital health.[9]

You didn't see Joseph being pessimistic about the setting God had him in. Nor did you see him being critical. This is the second thing he didn't do. Even when family scorned him and friends walked out on and forgot him, or when he was railroaded into a wrongful conviction, he kept his eyes focused forward on a living God who loved him and had a future for him.

That's not because he was a pacifist or didn't actively try to change his circumstances. (He denied the accusation that he had attempted to sleep with Potiphar's wife, and he sought help from a friend in prison to get him out.) But during those seasons of pain, he kept a crucial perspective: Joseph felt so strongly that God was directing his *outward* circumstances that he was free to concentrate on his *internal* state. Joseph's faith in almighty God allowed him to avoid not only pessimism but also another mark of emotional freeze points.

Freeze points can cause "pessimism bias."

Freeze points are those long-term trails that can affect our ability to love or feel loved. As time and again we feel our hopes are dashed with an ongoing trial, it can also freeze our sense of a positive outcome. Proverbs 13:12 captures this thought: "Hope deferred makes the heart sick, but a longing fulfilled is a tree of life" (NIV).

If we've gone through season after season of hurt or loss, it's understandable how we can end up with what's called a *pessimism bias,*[10] meaning if we've been through ongoing, repeated struggles, it can cause us to feel that's the norm. Things aren't going to get better, so why even try to see some new outcome? It's useless to create a LifeMap or believe there is help or hope beyond the difficult season we're experiencing.

Again, a look at Joseph in Scripture might presuppose that he'd have developed such a pessimism bias. After all, he'd been abused and abandoned by family and sold into slavery. Then he was unjustly accused and thrown in jail. Another difficult season followed where he was forgotten by friends whom he'd asked for help. That's one disheartening, freeze-point-chilling season after another—times when his efforts didn't seem to bring any reward or rescue.

Yet Joseph never quit looking forward. His unshakable view that God had a purpose, even in those difficult and repeated seasons of hurt, led him to recount to his brothers in Genesis 50:20, "You meant evil against me, but God meant it for good in order to bring about this present result, to keep many people alive."

An amazing verse regarding Jesus' learning through difficult times is Hebrews 5:8: "Although He was a Son, He learned obedience from the things which He suffered." We don't think about Jesus, God's own Son, learning from things. But with the hundreds of people we've helped process their own difficult freeze point experiences, a constant theme is their recounting things they learned through a difficult season—things like resilience, fortitude, faith, and hope.

Like Joseph, the truly optimistic person is empowered by the future and actively seeks to move and look toward it. And for the Christian, the future is our calling! "In My Father's house are many rooms" (John 14:2). "'For I know the plans that I have for you,' declares the LORD, 'plans . . . to give you a future and a hope.'" (Jeremiah 29:11). "Reaching forward to what lies ahead . . ." (Philippians 3:13).

We can be active in moving toward the future because it's a positive place when Jesus is in the picture—even if today we're in prison as Joseph was. That's the third thing Joseph didn't do: He didn't let his circumstances lead to procrastination instead of positive action. And that's the healthy perspective we ought to have. But emotional freeze points result in fear of the future and push us toward procrastination. Why is that? As we've seen, the more pessimistic you are about having a positive future, the lower your motivation to make changes today. And the greater fear you have trapped inside you that things will never change, the more you'll put off working your way out of problems and toward helpful goals.

Doctors Jane B. Burka and Lenora M. Yuen have written a helpful book on this subject called *Procrastination: Why You Do It, What to Do about It Now*. While I didn't actually finish the book, the parts I did read were very helpful. (Just kidding—I did finish the book . . . finally.)

In their studies of confirmed procrastinators, the authors saw this consistent fact: Procrastination is purposeful.[11] In other words, while people may not realize it or want to admit it, when they slow down or avoid doing even the most necessary things—like taking their high-blood-pressure medicine or making their mortgage payment—there's a purposeful decision to *not* do those things. And where does that decision to *not* step forward come from? It grows out of one of four types of fear: fear of failure, fear of success, fear of being controlled, or fear of intimacy.

Think back to those cards that are under Freeze Points on your LifeMap. Did any of those events lead you to experience any one of those types of fear? Like Jamie, did a fear of failure keep you hanging on to a destructive relationship when you should have let go? Has the fear of success, with its elevated expectations, kept you from finishing the school degree that is all that stands between you and a big promotion? Many of us fear being controlled by others—especially if we've felt the cold steel boot of being in an overcontrolling situation. And still others grow up fearing intimacy, particularly if they've regularly experienced distance, not closeness.

Emotional freeze points can damage your health and ruin important relationships by making you a pessimist. Then when you add fear to that toxic mix, it can make you a pessimistic procrastinator. But Joseph was neither, nor did he suffer from the next malady commonly linked with emotional freeze points.

Freeze points cause us to play God.

This indication of an emotional freeze point means taking it upon yourself to be judge, jury, and executioner rather than leaving that to God.

Not long ago, I (Kari) counseled a woman named Linda.

Her freeze point was created in the years she put up with a physically abusive father. A great sheet of emotional ice had made her so hard and impenetrable that her husband had recently left her, and even her lucrative job was teetering on the rocks.

Finally, during a counseling session, I confronted her about the venom that poured forth when the issue of her father, now deceased, came up. I asked if she had ever forgiven him.

"Forgive him?" she almost screamed at me. "I will never forgive my father. *I will overcome him. Do you hear me? I will overcome him!*"

With that, she got up, walked out of the office, and never came back.

What a tragedy! And what an example of an emotional freeze point! She had decided her layer of hurt couldn't be thawed out by love, only beaten to pieces by hate. But in every case—no exceptions—we're the ones who end up broken when we try to out-hate others. And good luck especially with trying to out-hate someone who is now a memory, with no chance of making changes.

> She had decided her layer of hurt couldn't be thawed out by love, only beaten to pieces by hate.

There's a reason the Scriptures tell us to love our enemies, not hate them. Namely, when we hold on to anger and hurts, we don't diminish our enemies' power over us—we increase it. We actually empower their hold on our lives when we try to play God and take judgment in our own hands.

Not that it wouldn't feel good to execute "righteous retribution" on an abusive father or someone who harmed our spouse or children. But God has established institutions like governments and civil authorities to carry out His punishment, for otherwise we carry their sentence within ourselves as well.

If you find you can't forgive someone who laid down a layer of hurt in your life, then like it or not, you're playing God. Not following God—playing God. And our God is a jealous God. He refuses to share His prerogatives with you, just as He refused to share them with an angel named Satan, who was much more qualified than you or me to play the part.

There was just one person who could play God with others because He was God. Picture the following scene.

A rowdy crowd was working its way down the street, pushing a young woman in front of it. She was probably scantily clad, which in itself in this culture that prided itself on covering up caused a stir among the many gathering to watch the boisterous procession.

Then, of all things, the crowd cast this woman in front of a carpenter from Nazareth. "Teacher," they told Him, "this woman has been caught in the very act of committing adultery. Now in the Law, Moses commanded us to stone such women; what then do You say?" (John 8:4-5).

We don't know if her actions were the result of a Pharisaic setup or her individual choices. Either way, the religious leaders certainly felt her actions provided them with a great opportunity to trap Jesus. If He rejected Moses' words, as they anticipated, they could brand Him as a lawbreaker and have Him written off.

That's when the same hands that worked in a woodshop as a young man and crafted the heavens ages before began to write on the ground. We don't know what words Jesus wrote. Perhaps He spelled out *envy, lust, lying, hypocrisy.*

The Bible says they "persisted" in pressing Him for an answer (John 8:7). They kept taunting Him: "What do You say? What's Your reply?" We don't know how long they kept at Him, but we do know what Jesus did when He straightened up. He spoke words that rang out like thunder in their ears.

Here was a band of angry, intense, intelligent men who felt they had Jesus trapped as tightly as a chess master traps a novice. But with one move, Jesus showed who was King, and He went from check to checkmate.

Jesus said, "He who is without sin among you, let him be the first to throw a stone at her" (John 8:7).

With that, He stooped down and went back to His writing.

Most of us are familiar with this New Testament story. The Scriptures record that beginning with the oldest (who had had the most time to accumulate sins) and down to the youngest, they all left. Every one of them.

While this is a great story of Jesus' compassion and mastery of the moment, what does it have to do with our discussion? A lot. Namely, it's what happened after the people had all left that speaks to the "playing God" trait of an emotional freeze point.

Jesus straightened up for a second time and said, "'Woman, where are they? Did no one condemn you?' She said, 'No one, Lord.' And Jesus said, 'I do not condemn you, either. Go. From now on do not sin any longer'" (John 8:10-11).

Do you hear the clear message behind His words?

She wasn't safe when the crowd left. There was still someone who could have picked up a rock. There was one person who was without sin and could have crushed her skull as the angry mob had wanted to do. But He didn't. As God,

He had the authority, purity, and right. But He chose to forgive her and send her on her way with the challenge to live a pure life.

One of the lessons from this passage is that judgment is best left to God. There have been times (as with Sodom and Gomorrah) when God has struck down entire cities. But in this case, God Himself in human form suspended judgment and issued forgiveness.

Can we do less? Forgiveness isn't the easy way of melting a freeze point, but it's essential in doing so. The primary New Testament word for *forgiveness* literally means to "untie the knot." Guess who stays tied up in knots if we *don't* forgive?

Turning a Blowtorch on Emotional Freeze Points

If you've experienced a season of hurt that has frozen your emotions, it does no good to slip into pessimism, procrastination, and playing God. Rather, like Joseph, you need to maintain an optimism rooted in the knowledge that God is in control of all circumstances—even the ones you have on cards on your storyboard.

When you face your fear of failure, success, being controlled, or intimacy, you throw rock salt on a freeze point, and your life becomes marked by responsibility and accountability, not procrastination. And finally, you turn a blowtorch on that layer of ice when you can actually do the godly thing and forgive those who have wronged you.

Sound easy? It couldn't have been for Joseph, particularly on a day when he had those same brothers (who had sold him down the river) up a creek without a paddle.

The strength to drop the stone

Joseph's father, Israel, had just died, and his brothers' guilty consciences began working overtime. "What if Joseph holds a grudge against us and pays us back in full for all the wrong which we did to him!" they asked themselves (Genesis 50:15). So they groveled before Joseph and asked him to forgive them for their transgression against him.

Joseph's response? Up to that point, he had done everything just the way Jesus would have done—but now could have been an exception.

If there was one man who deserved to throw stones at his brothers—the same ones who had been willing to stone him and sentence him to the rock pile of slavery—it was Joseph. Yet when it came time to pick up a rock (or to call for the palace guards and have his brothers slain, which he certainly had the power to do), he chose the harder path—the one Jesus would take Himself. ("Father, forgive them; for they do not know what they are doing" [Luke 23:34].)

> But Joseph said to them, "Do not be afraid, for am I in God's place? As for you, you meant evil against me, but God meant it for good in order to bring about this present result, to keep many people alive. So therefore, do not be afraid; I will provide for you and your little ones." So he comforted them and spoke kindly to them.
>
> GENESIS 50:19-21

Wow! What an example of someone who had every right to blame an emotional freeze point for an unfulfilled life!

What a temptation to put himself in God's place and become an agent of judgment rather than offer an act of healing!

As his brothers stood before him, Joseph had been the prisoner for years. But that day, he was freer inside than any of them, even to the point of being willing to provide for their little ones.

The Hardest Cards to Put Up . . . or Take Down

I know how hard it is to put cards on a storyboard that identify emotional freeze points. Do you remember those things I put on my LifeMap?

I also know it's possible to take them down. To extend forgiveness when what you've wanted to do is extend a left hook. To let God be the judge and take the higher road of forgiveness—and freedom.

I wish I hadn't had an unfaithful father who left a wife and three children under the age of three (when I was an infant). I'd love to have back all the time I spent questioning why he left. I would gladly have traded in being stood up by him the first time I was to meet him as a teenager (the "Traumatic first meeting" card on my LifeMap). It still hurts to think that for more than thirty years, I prayed, worked, and hoped for a positive relationship, only to have him die angry and indifferent, not knowing my younger daughter's name and caring less. The pain of those experiences led, in turn, to the card at the bottom of my freeze-points column: "Unwilling to let others truly get close."

I wish I didn't have a single card under this Freeze Point category in my LifeMap. These cards are not fresh and clean like the ones charting a positive future, nor are they filled with happy memories like those picturing strengths and successes.

But they're a part of my LifeMap, and you may have similar ones.

However, they're not all there is to our LifeMaps.

We can move on to look at other aspects of our past and to build a positive future. Through our own growth, we can even influence the next generation so they won't have to put rows of cards under Emotional Freeze Points on their LifeMaps years from now.

We've looked at successes and strengths and now emotional freeze points. Next up—individual flash points, the third element of LifeMapping.

Digging Deeper

1. After reading chapter 6, how would you define an *emotional freeze point*? Describe an emotional freeze point from your life.

2. Dr. Trent looked at potential freeze points in the life of Joseph (you can read his story in Genesis 37–50). In your own words, describe why the traumatic events in Joseph's life didn't turn into emotional freeze points.

3. If you haven't already done so, take the time now to fill out the emotional freeze points section of your LifeMap.

4. Read Matthew 18:21-35. Forgiveness is critical in order to overcome emotional freeze points. Is there anyone you need to forgive right now? Is anything preventing you from doing that? If you're stuck at this point, to whom can you go for help?

CHAPTER 7

Individual Flash Points

OUR GOD-GIVEN STRENGTHS can evolve over a lifetime. Emotional freeze points typically develop over a season. But this third LifeMapping element doesn't measure time in decades or even days. Individual flash points can arrive with the suddenness of a lightning flash or sonic boom. In fact, that's one of their characteristics. A flash point is often a lightning-bolt, one-time occurrence that happens in a moment yet carves out a new direction we may end up traveling for years—or a lifetime.

In this chapter, we'll look at the characteristics that individual flash points share and at the incredible power they have to rocket your life story forward or backward. And while individual flash points can pop up as suddenly as a Texas tornado, they can also be captured and recorded on a LifeMap.

For some people, flash points may involve a traumatic event with tragic consequences, like the sudden loss of a loved one. For others, they may be something positive, like the moment a friendship turns into real love and you realize that person sitting next to you is the one you're going to spend a lifetime with. Both are important to capture here. Let's start with a glimpse of the life-changing power of flash points.

Also, please note that while the flash point I'm about to describe wasn't as exciting as an explosion or lightning bolt—it was just a few simple words, quietly spoken by a casual friend—it nonetheless had an immediate, lasting impact on my mother's life and, indirectly, on my own.

Keeping a Friend from Falling through the Cracks

The year was 1952. For my mother, it was a time of heartache, pain, and transition. Less than six months earlier, my father had walked out the door, leaving her to raise and support a two-year-old (my older brother, Joe) and a set of two-month-old twins (my brother Jeff and me).

It's tough being a single parent today, but it was just as challenging in the 1950s. The new world she faced didn't look at divorce the way today's society does, as an acceptable option. There were no WIC programs for women with babies, no alimony, no family money to lessen the blow. And this was long before anyone got serious about holding "deadbeat dads" accountable, so not a dime of the court-ordered child support would ever come from my father.

Without a college degree or any job experience, Mom was suddenly required to raise three rambunctious boys while holding down a full-time clerical job. But she knew she needed more than the pittance she received for filing papers to keep four mouths fed. That's why she felt so strongly that if she were to make ends meet or ever move us ahead, she had to attend business school.

During her first days there, she had a horrible time mastering the fundamental business skill of typing. She had an even more difficult time with her typing teacher. Recently retired from the Army, he grilled and pushed his students like a drill sergeant with a sore tooth. And it seemed to my mother that he particularly delighted in tormenting her.

He relished pulling wadded papers from her trash can. He'd glance at the crumpled papers filled with errors. Then he'd thunder at her that she'd never be a good typist and how she ought to spare everyone the trouble, especially him, and just quit the class.

His teaching method, intimidation, might have worked in boot camp. But added to all the pressures of work and home, his scare tactics only made Mom's efforts more error prone. And what made it worse was that typing was a required part of her curriculum.

Mom couldn't skip over the class. She couldn't avoid his barrages. And she couldn't seem to make her fingers work fast enough to ever please him. That's why one night, after a particularly vicious outburst at the end of class, she was left with her head down, fighting back tears.

Everyone else had left the room when the pressure finally overwhelmed her. *It's just not working*, she said to herself, hot tears falling on her sweater. *Maybe I should quit.* And that's when a classmate suddenly appeared at her side.

The woman was just a casual acquaintance who had

walked back by the classroom and saw my mother sitting there. Mom had said hi to her in the hallway but didn't even know her last name. Nonetheless, this kindhearted friend gently put her hand on my mother's shoulder. And then she said something that would lift the gloom and set the course of Mom's life for the next thirty years.

"Honey," came a soft, Southern voice from a round, pretty face, "you just hang in there, ya hear? He's just putting on airs. You remember this, Zoa: You're going to make it. You're special. . . . And starting tomorrow, you fold those papers you're throwing away before you put them in the basket. That way they don't stack up so much, and he won't bother you— just watch."

> **She said something that would lift the gloom and set the course of Mom's life for the next thirty years.**

With that, she was gone. But that evening—with Mom at the end of her rope—God had brought to my mother someone who was barely a friend yet whose words hit her life at just the right time. Simple words. Quietly spoken. But seven words that surely came from God's heart:

"You're going to make it. You're special."

No one in the building heard a lightning bolt strike that night . . . except my mother. Her friend's words were a heavenly shot of encouragement at the very moment she was running up the white flag and ready to surrender.

With renewed hope (and now folding each paper she threw away), Mom did come back the next day. She worked harder than ever at the speed and accuracy tests the teacher barked out. Then came the moment of reckoning when she knew she was in harm's way.

There was her teacher, slowly moving down each row and finally rumbling to a stop at her desk like a Sherman tank. But this time, instead of turning the turret and blasting away at her, he paused—and gave her his first backhanded compliment. After grudgingly inspecting her wastebasket, he said, "I guess Zoa is finally getting with things."

Then he walked away to torment some other paper wadder.

Sometimes the smallest things become huge levers that shift the balance and direction of our lives—like a friend taking the time to walk over and offer brief words of hope and a simple suggestion like folding error-filled papers.

I'm proud to say that my mother graduated from business school with flying colors, and besides being a great mom, she enjoyed a wonderful career in the savings and loan field (long before its fall). In fact, she became so accomplished that as a businesswoman in 1959, she rated an ink sketch and article about her method for opening new branch offices on *The Wall Street Journal*'s front page!

But by her own account, none of that would have happened if she'd quit that night in 1952. What she realized in looking back on her life was that she had been hit by an individual flash point made up of seven simple words that changed her life forever.

That's the power of a flash point.

In some cases, it may be bold and brassy, like a row of trumpets or the clash of the cymbals. In other cases, it's as muted as the clarinet section or as quiet as a single light touch to a triangle. But flash points do have four things in common. Let's look at those characteristics now.

Moving from Darkness to Light

To illustrate the four traits, let's turn to a dramatic section of Scripture. There we find a man named Saul, who felt he was on a mission from God. His orders: Track down, arrest, and kill those claiming the name of Jesus, those "Christians" who were followers of the "Way" (see Acts 9:2).

He had gone to the authorities to obtain permission to make a list of those in Damascus who belonged to this sect. There would be no mercy. The names Saul collected were of people he was convinced were a plague, and he had a paper giving him power to sentence them to death.

But a funny thing happened on his way to exterminate more "heretics." He was hit by one of the most well-known individual flash points in history—with a blinding heavenly light.

> As he was traveling, it happened that he was approaching Damascus, and suddenly a light from heaven flashed around him; and he fell to the ground and heard a voice saying to him, "Saul, Saul, why are you persecuting Me?" And he said, "Who are You, Lord?" And He said, "I am Jesus whom you are persecuting, but get up and enter the city, and it will be told to you what you must do."
> ACTS 9:3-6

What happened to Saul (later referred to in Scripture as Paul) and what happened to my mother were worlds apart in scope and importance. Yet they do share and underscore those four things that characterize individual flash points.

A flash point happens suddenly.

The book of Acts is the account of the founding of the early church. As such, it chronicles the workings of God's Spirit in launching the gospel worldwide. What's more, it highlights the suddenness with which God often broke into people's lives:

- the sudden sound that filled the room at Pentecost
- the sudden appearance of the blinding light with Saul
- the sudden appearance of an angel who freed Peter from prison and led him to safety
- the sudden earthquake that freed Paul and Silas

There's a reason for the many sudden occurrences in the book of Acts: It's a history of God at work in the lives of His people, and He often works in decisive and dramatic ways.

That's the first aspect of an individual flash point. It usually doesn't come after twenty warm-up pitches or a long preseason. It comes suddenly, in a place as private as a practice rink, like the unexpected swing of a baton that smashed Nancy Kerrigan's knee to try to keep her out of the Olympics. Silver medal aside, her life would never be quite the same after that event. And neither would Tonya Harding's.

Or it's those unforgettable pictures from 9/11 of planes purposely hitting the Twin Towers in full view of cameras and millions of heartbroken people. That's the nature of a flash point. It often catches you off guard.

A flash point is unplanned.

Two years ago, Mike was a critical player in a major Austin tech firm. He was told over and over how indispensable he was because he was the only in-house person handling the entire firm's pension work.

Two days after the latest such assurance, Mike just knew that when they brought his name up at the annual partners' meeting, it would be to recommend him for partnership. Little did he know that instead of facing up to fourth-quarter losses and cutting partnership shares, they would decide to cut staff instead. And in a matter of minutes, Mike went from essential to expendable. When 9:00 a.m. rolled around the next business day, instead of working on his pension fund, he needed to draw on it after being let go.

Without a doubt, that was the most sudden and dramatic personal and vocational change Mike has gone through. Today, several years later, Mike owns and runs a fast-food establishment in a local mall.

Who'd have thought it? Four years of college. Three times struggling with and finally passing the CPA exam. He was trained to do books, not man a grill or bus tables. And now he isn't even the one doing the accounting. He's the one selling sushi and wonderful wok-cooked food.

If a flash point is marked by suddenness, it's also characterized by unexpectedness. It's something that leaves us saying, "Can you believe that happened?" "I never would have expected it in a million years!" "That's the last thing I'd have chosen."

I'm sure more heads were turning in Damascus at Saul's sudden conversion than at a tennis tournament. From exterminator to evangelist. From a committed Pharisee to a preacher of the Cross. Who'd have expected it? And yet it's so like God.

Who would have sent a young boy with a slingshot to face a giant except God? Who could have come up with a huge fish submarine to transport Jonah where he needed to be but God? Who else would have expected the King of kings and Lord of lords to be born in a stable, laid in a manger, and looked over by shepherds?

Dennis Byrd was a tremendous professional football player and a marvelous person. But one play, one crushing collision, left him not only sidelined but also immobilized. His dramatic struggle to recover is chronicled in his outstanding book *Rise and Walk*, but his experience was and is a dramatic example of the unexpected nature of life.

A flash point is often unexplainable.

Why did my friend Dave Dravecky, a former Major League Baseball pitcher, work so hard to come back from cancer and end up not only losing a career but also his arm? Why did that officer on Oahu fail to heed the radar warnings on December 7, 1941, that a mass of unidentified airplanes was coming toward Pearl Harbor?

There's an element of God's dealing in our lives that remains unexplainable, unfathomable. But that doesn't mean He's erratic or unprincipled like the mythical gods of Olympus. Rather, almighty God reserves the right to alter any life story in the blink of an eye, no matter how carefully we've planned it out.

My twin brother, Jeff, and his family were at Candlestick Park in San Francisco the night Dave made his incredible comeback from cancer. They have the ticket stub he signed after winning the game and a picture he sent them with a verse he treasures. But in spite of Dave's courage and the love and support of his wife, Jan, his arm snapped in a split second a few days later.

It's hard to understand the dramatic nature of some individual flash points. But in the message of Dave and Jan's outstanding book *When You Can't Come Back*, it's clear that we can trust God even if all the logical reasons don't add up.

A flash point is individual.

When Saul was driven to the ground by the heavenly light surrounding the risen Jesus he persecuted, others stood "hearing the voice but seeing no one" (Acts 9:7). While millions of viewers might have seen the play that broke Dennis Byrd's spine or the one that snapped Dave Dravecky's arm, there was an element of even those public experiences reserved only for the individuals. To some other person, in some other setting, the words my mother heard might have meant little or nothing. For her, they held tremendous individual encouragement.

A flash point, then, may or may not be something remarkable to another person who observes it. But from a personal standpoint, while you don't know all the ramifications in that instant, deep inside there's still a realization that your life has undergone a major change.

■

Sudden. Unplanned. Unexplainable. Individual.

Those are four marks of a flash point. And like the three LifeMapping elements before this, you can capture them as part of your life story. You may be thinking, however, *The others I can see, but this one I'm sure is a blank. I've never been visited by angels, won a medal on TV, or had anything dramatic happen to me.*

But remember, the operative word with a flash point isn't necessarily *drama* but *direction*.

> **The operative word with a flash point isn't necessarily *drama* but *direction*.**

Can you think of a time when someone said or did something and it challenged or changed the direction of your life? Did a single event, or perhaps even several, come ringing through that pushed aside all your priorities at the time and suddenly gave you a new set of hurdles to face?

Let's look at several other examples of flash points that might help you identify some cards for your storyboard. For some, a flash point will often come out of a first-time experience. For others, it will be something incredibly positive. And for still others, it may be the most shameful thing they've ever faced.

Where to Look for Individual Flash Points

Sometimes, your first-time experience at something can become a flash point for you. For example, someone may pick up a guitar for the first time and just know that playing it is something he or she was *meant* to do.

Our family had the great honor of being friends with Medal of Honor winner Joe Foss, a Marine pilot and leading fighter ace of World War II. I remember Joe telling me about when he decided he'd become a pilot. He grew up on a farm, and one time, as a young boy, he climbed to the very top of a tall windmill. He had never been that high before—and when his mother saw him, that was also the last time he climbed that windmill. But that was it. That feeling of being up in the sky never left him and led him to become a pilot.

Yet sometimes, that flash point can push us away from something, like a career we might have been good at. Consider Dr. Seuss.

Theodor Seuss Geisel (later to be called Dr. Seuss) was born in 1904, and as a young man, he was witty and out-going with friends. Such verbal strengths might have led him into business, sales, or even drama—but not after an incident that happened when he was thirteen.

During World War I, Geisel's Boy Scout troop sold a record number of war bonds, and the boys were to be presented with medals by former president Theodore Roosevelt. Geisel's troop sat on the stage as Roosevelt praised them and called out their names one by one.

Finally, young Theodor was left alone on the stage with Roosevelt. The former president searched his list and then glared at the embarrassed boy. "What is this little boy doing here?" he said.

Unfortunately, Geisel's name had been inadvertently omitted from the list. Years later, explaining why he always felt insecure in crowds and seldom gave speeches, he recalled the shame: I can still hear them whispering, 'There's little Teddy Geisel, he tried to get a medal.' And to this day I keep asking myself, 'What *am* I doing here?'"[1]

Facing a crowd may have caused some to step forward. It caused Dr. Seuss to retreat from public speaking and teaching. But how that flash-point experience benefited him and millions of others! Geisel's redirected efforts went into writing and illustrating children's books, bringing joy to millions of fans. (All this from a man whose teacher told him that he would never succeed as an artist if he always broke the conventional rules of drawing and whose Dartmouth College classmates voted him "least likely to succeed"!)

First Class . . . Lifelong Direction

Both cards on my LifeMap are connected to a first experience I had in seminary. In fact, one card came out of the same class in which Dr. Hendricks gave us the strengths test I mentioned earlier.

During registration the week before school started, I was wading through lines of students who, like me, were scurrying to fill their class schedules. A friend grabbed me and said, "Hey, they're switching to the auditorium for Dr. Hendricks's class on the Christian home, so more seats have opened up. Come on and sign up with me."

My friend was married, and he and his wife were expecting their second child any day. I was single and so broke and busy, just getting a date would have been exciting. Why in the world did I need to sign up for Christian Home?

But I needed an elective, and I'd heard how hard it was to get into Dr. Hendricks's classes. So I followed my friend to register. I stood up at the end of the first class session with the unshakable conviction that I had found the direction God wanted for my ministry and life from that point forward. That led me to walk to that pay phone, call my mother, and explain everything to her.

That class was a flash point for me. It redirected my life and reoriented the compass that would lead me.

How about you? Has your life taken momentous turns that have shaped your future?

God Does Pivotal Things in Everyday People's Lives

I don't know what cards will go under your list of individual flash points. My friend Stu Weber described to me two of his flash-point cards. You can read about both of them in his excellent book *Tender Warrior*. One flash point came when he was a Green Beret in Vietnam, when he jumped out of a plane and his parachute didn't open! The other was the day his wife, Linda, told him he wasn't measuring up as a husband and father.

Your flash point may be something as dramatic as the sound the wind makes when you're falling at one hundred twenty miles an hour and your parachute won't open or as quiet as words of correction that shake you to your very core. But it's likely that you have had some watershed events in your life that your LifeMap can capture. And once you have those on your map, you're ready to make one more stop to tie up loose ends from your past.

That *One* Post under Flash Points

Is a post under this element of LifeMapping really that significant? For one woman I counseled, it was far more than significant.

As I talked about flash points, her mind went back to a time when she lived in military base housing in South Carolina. She'd just gotten home from school one day. Her mother had left a note saying she was at the store and would be back soon. That's when the doorbell rang.

She walked to the front door, opened it, and there were the base commander and the base chaplain—a sight no one living on an Army base ever wants to see. Her father had been killed in Afghanistan. Her mother came home, heard the news, and fell apart emotionally. Within three months, she had shipped her daughter out to her grandparents. A year later, the girl's mother died of what her daughter was told was an accidental overdose.

Now an adult in my counseling office, the woman had in front of her probably one hundred cards picturing her life story on her LifeMap storyboard. But she walked up to that one card under Individual Flash Points.

"It's so clear," she said.

"There was *before* the doorbell rang . . . and *after*. I've tried a million times to unsee the two of them standing there at the door. And seeing Mom fall apart for the first time.

"But this is the first time I can see that that's only one card. My life really is more than just that terrible day."

Amen. And if a flash-point card of yours carries that much weight, so does your life. Like Mary, who picked up the note in the first chapter. Or people who walk out of the doctor's office having heard, "Stage four." Flash points, good and bad, can indeed be powerful moments.

Next, we'll look at yet another group of memories and experiences, what I call untied transitions.

Digging Deeper

1. Use your own words to describe a flash point.

2. Write down one positive and one negative flash point from your own life and how each affected you.

3. If you haven't already done so, fill out the flash-point cards for your LifeMap.

4. Can you recall a time when God used a negative flash point to redirect your life in a positive way? Describe what happened. How can this help you deal with future negative flash points?

CHAPTER 8

Untied Transitions

WE CAN FACE all kinds of transitions in life—going from grade school to high school; from single to married or from married to single; from parent to grandparent; from employed to unemployed. In each transition, there is great potential for positive change or for being unable to make needed changes.

All the potential positive things and potential problems that transitions bring constitute this fourth element of the LifeMapping process. That's why, in this chapter, we'll take a close look at the four major types of transitions we all face and at the three phases we must go through when they happen. We'll see how God designed us to deal with transitions and how we can gain an edge on many of them by anticipating and preparing for their often-known-in-advance arrival.

Not sure what I mean by a transition? Consider Kensie, who started early in life having to make huge transitions.

No Time to Grieve

Kensie was ten years old when she started hearing all the hushed conversations. Her mother and father were talking in low tones so the children couldn't hear. Her mother started being gone for several days at a time. But then came the day she finally came home for good, and there was no hiding what was happening. Kensie's mother was dying. And plans were being made and huge changes swirled around Kensie in those brief last three months.

As if the death of her mother weren't transition enough, her father—without any discussion with Kensie or her brother and sister—remarried seven months later. The woman he married had six children of her own, making a total of eleven people in a home that had seemed crowded with just three kids and their parents.

Years had passed when Kensie did her LifeMap. Yet this element of LifeMapping was by far the most difficult—but also the most helpful. It brought back all those challenging memories. But it also explained so much about why she struggled when any changes were made to her life or schedule.

Essentially Different from a Flash Point

"But wait a minute, John," you may say. "Aren't we talking about the same thing as in the last chapter? Isn't a flash point the same as an untied transition?"

It's true that a flash point can forcibly evict you from one season of life, ushering you into times of significant change. But while some transitions come with the suddenness of a flash point, many more arrive at glacial speed. For example, there is hardly an instant flash between turning twenty and turning forty. But both are huge transition points—moving out of the teens and moving into midlife. Each signals major changes that need to be accepted and processed.

In many ways, flash points could be likened to a wedding, marking the day a transition started. But the quality of the marriage that results will reflect how the couple actually dealt with that transition. So while there may be some overlap, let's look at a definition of a transition that might further clarify what is meant.

Defining a Time of Transition

The definition: *Untied transitions* are major movements in your life, often outside your control, that usher in a new season of life or a new way of relating. They're a closing off of the old, and if left untied, they cause us to face a future only in light of what's unfinished or untied.

A good way to look at major transitions is to view them as mini rites of passage. A flash point may take you to a point of transition, but how successfully you deal with the new set of rules will determine if you pass through it successfully or remain stuck and stymied by it. Let me illustrate with an example from one of the most beautiful places in the United States.

Several years ago, I had the chance to meet a precious family who lives on Kodiak Island, Alaska. (I'll admit that doing a conference in Alaska is a tough job, but somebody's got to do it!) Craig and Terrie Johnson were our seminar coordinators for the Love Is a Decision seminar Gary Smalley and I held there. And they were also our fishing guides five minutes after the seminar ended.

I'll never forget flying in a seaplane to a smaller island called Afognak and fishing for salmon up and down a beautiful river. Salmon fishing is serious business in Alaska, and at one point along the river, we came across a cabin next to a salmon gate (called a weir).

There in the middle of the wilderness, a state game and fish employee was manning this gate, accompanied by his wife and three small children. (The gatekeeper and his wife, Cort and Katrina Neff, turned out to be members of Craig and Terrie's home church.) I'd never seen a salmon gate before, but essentially, it represents a transition point for migrating salmon. It also provides a picture of what transitions can mean to you.

When salmon are hatched in those beautiful mountain streams, they stay in the shallows until they grow big enough, and then they travel downstream to the bay and finally out into the ocean. After they grow large and fearsome in the rough, cold Arctic waters, God turns on an internal homing signal that points them back to Afognak. In some cases, this means taking a journey of two thousand miles or more to end up in the very stream where they were born, and where they now seek to lay their eggs.

The salmon gate provides two services for the fish and fish managers. First, it allows the game and fish employee to count the number of salmon heading upstream (an incredible feat with the hundreds of salmon that congregate below the gate). That allows a forecast to be made of the number of salmon they expect to harvest that year. But the gate also provides a breathing place for the salmon to rest and gather strength before continuing the arduous journey upstream.

It was astounding to stand above the gate and look at the hundreds of salmon waiting for it to open. Milling around. Darting back and forth. Looking like carbon copies of those huge fish you see on the walls at Red Lobster or your uncle's house. And finally, when the gate opened, they shot through the opening and on toward their goal.

When the gates are wide open during the peak of their run, at times hundreds of fish will be jumping ahead, pushing forward . . . and yet some never do. For reasons as varied as sickness or choice, they stay right at the entrance to the gate, never taking that next step in their journey.

The same thing is true for all of us who face transitions in life.

Some people shoot with reckless abandon through each gate, marking a passage into another phase of life. Others do well with the first two or three gates, but then they can't seem to get beyond the fourth.

To help you determine some of those gates in your life, take a moment to write down the answers to four questions.

1. As you look at your life story, when would you say a new chapter opened up for you?
2. When would you say your childhood ended?
3. When was the first time you said to yourself, "I'm really on my own"?
4. What was it that made you ready to say, "It's time to settle down"?

Questions like these can help you picture some key transitions in your life, times that challenged you to adapt to events often not under your control. It's often someone else who opens and closes the gates you seek to go through. And each of the four major types of transitions can seem to have a life and mind of its own.

The Four Major Transitions That Can Shape Your LifeMap

Core relationships

Put your memory on rewind and think about your most important relationships since childhood. Your parents. Siblings, aunts, uncles, and grandparents. Then there are those core relationships you develop apart from your family. When any of those core relationships change, get ready for a transition—or in some cases, a place where you can get in an emotional whirlpool.

For example, I remember my grandfather passing away when I was just a boy. He died so quickly of a brain aneurysm that one minute he was standing with us in the living room, and the next he was gone. He had just moved in with us, and having grown up in a single-parent home, I was so looking forward to having a father figure. It had been a transition to switch rooms to make space for him and my grandmother. Now there was the transition of watching my grandmother grieve and not having him.

Then there was the transition that came on the night I held my father's hand, praying for him as he coughed his life away, and finally watching him slip away. And four years later, four doors down in the same hospice, my mother went to be with the Lord.[1]

It's not just death, of course, that can change our core relationships and force us into a time of transition. Sometimes it's brought on by a change in the quality of a person's life.

My mother was a wonderful person with an irrepressible spirit and contagious trust in God. Yet that pillar of strength was also a woman with rheumatoid arthritis who kept losing physical battles and having to transition from one level of movement and life to another. From walking briskly to struggling to walk. From driving a car to having her wrists hurt so much that she had to give it up. From using a walker to having to get in that mobile cart.

I marveled at the way my mother faced each of these transitions. The reality would break upon her. She wasn't going to get better. There was a new normal. She'd cry, sometimes for the better part of a day. But then she'd dry her face, and she'd begin to deal with that transition to a different set of life abilities. After that one good cry, it was back to that same irrepressible smile and uplifting spirit for everyone around her. She was the queen of making godly, helpful, hopeful, difficult transitions, even when they meant transitioning *down* a step, not *up* in terms of life or lifestyle.

What we can all know is that God stands at the gate of our core relationships. At times, the gate is open, and changes take place rapidly. And then there are times of quiet and waiting, periods when the gate is closed, and it seems things will never change. But deep inside, we know they will.

We're never really safe from a shift or change in core relationships. Even with a precious, pure-white American

Eskimo dog who hasn't changed his heartwarming smile in fourteen years. As I write this, I know the day will come when my heart is broken, and I have to transition from walking with him each night to walking without him.

Transitions might mean losing a parent; gaining a spouse in our twenties; ending a friendship in our forties; or laying a brother to rest in our sixties. Transitions are real and need to be talked through, not left untied, as hard as that can be.

Physical changes

Changes can also be physical in two senses of the word. First, there are those inevitable physiological changes you face with aging. On a basketball court, for example, those changes make you go from unstoppable at driving to the basket at nineteen to shooting from the outside at age thirty-five and letting those young guys crash the boards. They result in having more hair growing out of your ears than on your head in your forties (hopefully only if you're a man). And they make necessary that first serious visit to a doctor in your late fifties where you hear the dreaded word *colonoscopy*.

We all wear out. That's a tough reality to face. I learned it the hard way on my birthday some years ago.

I was out in the rugged mountain preserve where I regularly ride my mountain bike. It was the crack of dawn on a beautiful June morning. It was also my fortieth birthday, and I was feeling great. I was bombing down steep hills and cranking through the uphill parts without breaking a sweat.

I have a favorite course I've laid out, and I'd already made it through the steep, life-threatening part in record time. Now I was flying along on a wide, perfectly level trail on my way out of the preserve and toward the paved road home.

I had just thought what great shape I was in for a forty-year-old! That's when somehow, either a partly buried rock or a patch of gravel pushed my front tire slightly off the trail—and straight into trouble. With incredible timing, my tire slid right between two rocks that were half-buried and formed a perfect V.

As you can imagine, when my front tire hit that solid-rock V, the bike went from full speed to full stop instantly—only I didn't. I flew over my handlebars, crashed into the rocky ground, and rolled into a cholla cactus. (For those of you unfamiliar with the Sonoran Desert, cholla, or "jumping," cacti are the Arnold Schwarzeneggers of cacti! They're the mean ones you really don't want to mess with!)

With my bike helmet cracked in half (yes, I learned in that tumble that that's actually possible) and my body filled with burning cactus spikes, my mortality stared me right in the face. Even today, whenever I respectfully pass that part of my course, I always think about the living example God gave me of "Pride goeth before a fall."

No matter how fast you ride right now, the day will come when you take a fall. Your health, vitality, or eyesight will gradually fail, and when it does, it will bring on unquestioned transitions.

Physical can also refer to those major geographic or standard-of-living changes that can jar you as much as a poor EKG reading. I think of the woman I heard of recently who won $10 million in a state lottery, and within a single year she had lost all her money and her marriage as well. For her, physical changes meant going from a lower-middle-class home to life at the Ritz to ending up living out of a suitcase—all in one year!

I also think of Dane, who spent the first thirteen years

of his life in eighteen different grade schools because his father "liked to move around." For him, physical transitions reflected the ever-changing landscape of his youth, and because of the lack of roots, he struggles with settling down even today in spiritual and personal relationships.

Core relationships and physical changes may show up as cards on your LifeMap. So, too, may the third type of transition.

Vocational changes

For both men and women, vocational changes can be dramatic and traumatic. They often cause major adjustment problems, even if that transition is to retirement!

The average person retiring at age sixty-five can expect to live at least another ten years.[2] Then again, you may happen to be George "Bear" Bryant of Alabama football fame, and you die about *one month* after you stop coaching.

What about all the trailer trips across the country those folks talked about at work? What about those cries for days when there was nothing to do but bowl or go fishing?

For many men and women, retirement can mean the loss of a vocational definition of who they are—and that unprocessed vacuum can spell trouble for their lives and health.

Perhaps in the past year or two, you've been hired or fired from a job. That shuffling of the bread-and-butter role can play havoc with your life, and it needs to be represented on your LifeMap. And there's one further area of transition that should show up as well.

Spiritual changes

Each of us experiences spiritual transitions as well as relational and physical ones. Initially, we move from lost to found; from immature to mature; from milk to solid food. But some of us also move backward from mature to immature, like Dan.

Dan and his family were founding members of a small church with five other couples who first met in each other's homes. Today, only twelve years later, that same church sits on fourteen acres. With eight buildings, it carries more than two thousand families on its rolls.

Dan was the first elder. The first chairman of the elder board. The first building committee chairman. He was also the first board member to leave his wife of thirty years and move in with a woman one year younger than his oldest daughter.

Talk about a spiritual transition for him, his family, *and* his church family! Negative changes in your spiritual life can significantly affect you and set off changes in others as well. (Thankfully, many more people make positive spiritual changes instead.)

People don't usually take just one big step away from Jesus and Christlike living. It's much more like the church of Ephesus we looked at—they start strong but then start to drift away. The big step at the end is only the last step in a drawn-out process.

> **People don't usually take just one big step away from Jesus and Christlike living.**

Oscar's story showed up that way on his LifeMap. He'd started strong. But over time, he saw his spiritual vitality draining away. He found himself going through the motions and reaching for a close relationship with Christ, but never really taking hold of it.

As he went through this section of his LifeMap with his small group at church, however, he saw for the first time how his transition to a new job had devoured every spare second. That included time he couldn't afford to spare with his family and, especially, his spiritual life. He used to get up early and find time with the Lord. With the new position, he had to leave earlier and stay later, and there went any time for exercise, physically or spiritually.

One of the great things about doing a LifeMap is that once you post it, you can see it. And drawing out where we really are in the midst of transitions can be a great help in getting back to growing faith and family relationships.

Core relationships, physical changes, vocational shifts, and spiritual growth—these are four major areas in which transitions hit us. And when they do, they frequently bring with them a three-part challenge.

Three Challenges That Come with Each Transition

As you think back over your life story and some of the transitions you've already experienced, you'll quickly see the three steps, or phases, that come as an inescapable part of each turning point. It's as my old boss on the construction site used to say: "If you order Chinese food, you're *going* to get a fortune cookie." And if you experience a transition, you're inevitably *going* to face the following three challenges.

The phase of endings

While it may sound contradictory, transitions always begin with an ending. The apostle Paul said, "When I was a child, I used to . . . think like a child . . . ; when I became a man, I did away with childish things" (1 Corinthians 13:11).

Adulthood begins with the ending of youth. Marriage

marks the end of single life. Parenting signals the end of sleeping in. In each case, coming to grips with the fact that one way of life is ending and being replaced by another may not be easy. (But take heart. If endings were easy, there would be no country music!)

Can you remember when your children were young and you would throw them high into the air? While they'd scream bloody murder on the way up, what's the first thing they'd say after they landed safely back on earth? "Do it again! Do it again!"

No matter how often we ask, there are things in life that we can't do again, pages we can't turn back to except in our minds.

Can you imagine what it would have been like living in the last generation of ancient Romans before the fall of the empire? With the barbarians at the gates, they surely wondered why history had to change with them. Why they couldn't pass down to their children a culture that had been the world leader. But there wasn't to be a handoff for that last generation. They had outlived their season of glory, and there was no way they could revive it.

There comes a time when we have to put things down and admit that a particular period of time has passed.

I once heard the story of two monks who started on a long journey. It had rained hard the day before they left, and they rounded a corner and saw where the river had washed away a bridge. Standing beside the river was a beautiful woman dressed in an exquisite gown.

One of the monks cheerfully offered to carry her across the river so her dress would not be ruined. Lifting her into his arms, he waded across and deposited her safe and dry on the other side. With a polite word of thanks, the woman went on her way, and the monks continued their journey in a different direction.

They had just gotten out of earshot of the woman when the monk who had not carried the woman turned in anger on his companion.

"How could you do that?" he spat. "You know our order forbids interaction with women, and you held one close and carried her across the river!"

"Yes," said the other monk, "I carried her across and set her down. But it appears that you carry her still."

Many of us have things in our past that we can't seem to "put down." They stay lodged in our minds or held in our arms. But the fact is that while we may try to put an old title on a new book, it simply doesn't fit anymore. There are endings that need to be processed . . . and sometimes even grieved.

LAST FAREWELLS

I remember an ending I had to face up to. The year was 1972. I'd been up almost all night, first saying goodbye to high school friends and then packing for college. I sat at the old kitchen table with my mother and enjoyed her wonderful pancakes one last time before climbing into my jam-packed car.

As I sat there, a flood of emotions hit me. It was there I had sat as a five-year-old, laughing, clowning around, and spilling milk with my brothers. It was the same table where my grandfather had sat, looking out the window at us playing and giving us a smile and a wave of his hand. And it was one place I could sit with my mother day or night, and she would patiently listen to whatever crisis or problem I was having in school.

Over the years, the chairs around the table had begun to empty. My grandfather passed away, leaving a huge, open spot. My older brother, Joe, got married and had a table of his own to sit at. My twin brother, Jeff, had already left for a different college. And now it was down to Mom and me, sitting at that table one last time.

I remember how well I thought she was handling that morning when I was heading off to Texas Christian University, home of the mighty Horned Frogs.

No tears.

No dip in her always-present smile.

Just that nonstop encouragement that calmed my fears and made me feel as if I weren't driving 1,200 miles by myself or starting a whole new way of life; I was just heading off to class or down to Pete's Fish and Chips for a Coke.

I finished breakfast, hugged the best mom in the world, and confidently strode to my '64 forest green Volkswagen, every square inch crammed with important stuff for college. I fired up the engine, beeped the horn, and drove off into the sunrise with a wave and a smile.

I hadn't gone three miles down the road before I realized I'd forgotten my sunglasses.

In Arizona, when you drive off into the sunrise without sunglasses, you notice it. I'd left mine on my nightstand. I turned the car around, drove back into the driveway, and walked in to find my mother still sitting at the kitchen table, crying.

All morning, Mom had kept a stiff upper lip and managed to hold her emotions in check. Sure, she was seeing her last son leave home. But she felt that what he needed was confidence, not crying. Then I walked back in unexpectedly—and saw her sitting at the table.

That's all it took to open the floodgates. It was only the two of us who hugged, cried, and held each other, but suddenly the table was crowded with every family member who had gone on—and with hundreds of loving memories.

We finally stopped crying, and I drove to Texas to begin a new chapter of life. I never had breakfast with Mom at that table again. It went in a garage sale while I was off at school (along with my baseball card collection that could have paid for my college education today).

I can't tell you how many times I've wanted one more meal with all my family around the table. Grandma and Grandfather passing the food. My brothers and I laughing and cutting up, and Mom trying to keep three "starving" boys fed. But it won't happen again unless the Lord allows replays in heaven. (Isn't that a great thought?)

There are endings when a transition comes. And there's often a time of questioning as well.

The phase of questioning

I also recall facing another last-time-at-the-table experience. For nearly ten years, I had the privilege of working alongside Gary and Norma Smalley and their wonderful staff of people like Terry Brown, Roger Gibson, Greg Smalley, Jim Brawner, Kari Sumney, Penny Blanchard, Penni DeOrtinzio, Beth Selby, and many others in Phoenix.

In June 1993, however, they moved the ministry of Today's Family to Branson, Missouri. Now, Branson is the exact center of the United States (in terms of population distribution) and an excellent place to raise families and expand a ministry. You can even hook record-breaking fish, catch a different country music show every night of the week, and go to Silver Dollar City to boot!

But when the moving van pulled out for Missouri, Cindy and I didn't follow it. Moving to Branson would have meant leaving our home state and church, our kids' school, my mother, and Cindy's parents and family. It seemed clear, after much prayer about what God wanted us to do, that He was telling us to stay in Arizona.

My ten years of ministry with Today's Family came to a close when those moving vans pulled out, and so began a new ministry called Encouraging Words, which today is called StrongFamilies.com. And while I felt we were doing exactly what the Lord wanted us to do, that's not to say there weren't times when I questioned my next challenge.

Try building a counseling practice in mid-summer in Phoenix (when everyone suddenly leaves for Denver and San Diego). As many readers who have started a new business know, billions of details and hundreds of dollars go into setting up an office, even with a staff of only one. (There are also some advantages to working alone. For example, I got to take myself out to lunch for both Administrative Professionals' Day and Boss's Day—and I had a great time at both parties!)

In a few short months, I'd set up the ministry and launched a nationwide seminar on the Old Testament concept of "the blessing" (where I also taught about LifeMapping). With the encouragement and support of friends like Focus on the Family, I was already booked nearly two years out at churches across the country. I was busy writing children's books and relationship books, and even my small counseling practice was filled to overflowing.

But even that promising start didn't mean questions wouldn't crop up. And it didn't mean that I'd never think back to working and clowning around with Gary or about the fact that we could have been fishing and working together in Missouri.

Since the day I left seminary and joined a ministry team, I'd always had someone to grab for lunch. I'd always been part of a team where something was happening to someone that would bring a smile or elicit a word of support in the halls. There had always been someone to double the victories and help share the sorrows—that is, until now.

In a few short months, I'd gone from the center of a large beehive of activity and people to the incredibly quiet walls of a twelve-by-twelve office. I'd gone from walking down to the yogurt shop with a work friend, sometimes twice in one day, to eating lunch alone four or five days a week.

> I'd gone from walking down to the yogurt shop with a work friend, sometimes twice in one day, to eating lunch alone four or five days a week.

I wasn't complaining. God had blessed my family and new ministry in every way. But it's okay to question, too. That's a part of the transition process, and it may be the stage you're in right now.

I think of Kyle, whose wife left him two years ago, and he still can't piece together why. And of Lydia, who understood logically all the reasons for job cutbacks but still can't understand why she was the one cut.

You can truly believe, as I do, that you're right where God wants you. But there still may be that occasional "What if . . . ?" Thankfully, there's a third phase that helps in answering those questions. It's the phase that risks moving on.

The phase of taking steps to begin a new day

Before their honeymoon in Hawaii, a man and his wife-to-be decided to take scuba lessons together. That way, when they got to the islands, they could go out on a boat as a couple and enjoy diving among the coral and schools of beautifully colored fish.

They completed their lessons, had their wedding, and flew to Hawaii. They chartered a boat along with some other would-be divers, and everything was going according to plan—until they actually got to the place where they were to enter the water.

The boat had stopped in the transition swells created where an underwater coral reef and the open sea meet. The boat jerked and swayed, and the uneven chop of the water made it difficult to get suited up and get safely over the side. The swells had been so bad, my friend said, that he'd had to coax his new wife to climb into the water. Even when she got in, her eyes were still as big as saucers, and she refused to go under, instead bobbing up and down like a cork on the surface.

Afraid that she would be thrown against the boat and hit her head, he finally helped her put her mouthpiece in and pushed her underwater.

By dropping down a few feet, they experienced a remarkable change. They went from chaos and churning waters to an incredible calm. No more whipping wind. No more pounding waves. Just placid waters and a peaceful quiet.

That's a great picture of this third transitional phase you can capture in your LifeMap. Namely, when you take active steps in the face of transition and do something new, the waters often begin to grow quiet, and a sense of calm enters your life again.

In July 1993, I was so frazzled and worn out from my career transition that I wondered if I could ever make a change. But I was thankful for five couples who constituted the most supportive board any ministry could ever have. Most of all, I was thankful for an incredibly supportive wife who kept putting the mouthpiece in my mouth— reminding me to breathe and encouraging me to enjoy the plunge. It's amazing how the waters changed. From initial feelings of loneliness and being overwhelmed, I grew to love the freedom to create and build a whole new ministry. And while the transition waters were a bit rough, the seas calmed, and I felt right in the center of where God wanted me.

That's my encouragement to you. Perhaps you've got a number of cards on your LifeMap that represent major changes in core relationships, vocational shifts, or physical challenges. It's okay to question and, like Jesus, ask to put down some cups you've been handed; or like Paul, to pray that those thorns be removed. But as we look to our heavenly Father for strength, we'll also be able to take those first active steps in a new direction . . . and see the inner waters begin to calm down.

David is a man who went from successful entrepreneur to working for a huge company. He went from making instant decisions to waiting months before a single change he suggested was approved; from calling all the shots to waiting for someone else to make the call.

The waters were rough in making that change. But the major thing that helped him—and that helped me in starting our ministry—is looking at a God who never changes and trusting Him for the strength to make first steps.

David doesn't see his company changing much. The waters there are still choppy. But he knows he can trust God, lean back in the water, and find an inner place of quiet.

The Strength to Accept Transitions

From the Old Testament to the New, God's Word highlights one transition after another in the lives of His people. Adam and Eve certainly made a major transition in leaving the Garden. Abram trusted God as he left his homeland of Ur for the unknown. Peter went from being an eager supporter to swearing he didn't even know Jesus to being a rock. The Scriptures are filled with people who faced all the transitions we do—and many who faced them well.

We've already looked at Joseph and the incredible transitions he went through—all those changes of geography, vocation, and core relationships—without ever giving up trust in God or giving in to pessimism. And then there's the Lord Jesus Himself. If anyone modeled "closing the loop," it was Him. Just pick up your Bible and take a look at John 19. There you'll see three of His seven last statements from the cross.

He had faced the great battle at Gethsemane. He had prepared the disciples at the Last Supper. He had already forgiven His executioners. And then on the cross, He even provided for His mother's care. ("Woman, behold, your son! . . . [Son,] behold, your mother!" [John 19:26-27].)

As the Lord prepared to make the unfathomable transition from the very source of life to taking death upon Himself for us, He cried out, "I am thirsty" (John 19:28). That wasn't just a dying man's request for refreshment. Rather, He who is the living water was thirsting for the first time from eternity past for His Father's presence.

All that love, passion, and drama were then tied in a final knot when He cried out, "It is finished!" (John 19:30). That part of His work and life was done. The Son of God had died so that we who love Him would never have to taste spiritual death. His resurrection and future reign in heaven and on earth were still to come. But the ending of the Cross had to take place before the new beginning at the empty tomb.

Without the ending of His life, there would be no newness of life. Without Good Friday, there would be no Easter. Unless a grain first falls to the ground and dies, there's no stalk of life-sustaining wheat. That ending of Jesus' life opened up a whole new beginning for each of us who put our faith in Him alone as our Lord and Savior.

Let's face it, since the time of Abraham, God has called each of us to be "foreigners and strangers" (1 Peter 2:11). There isn't one of us who can tear down his barns to build new ones and be certain the Lord won't call him or her home before the job is done. We're all in transition. We were born for transition, born to move from darkness to light; from slavery to sonship; from childhood to adulthood; from living to dying; from a decaying earth to our heavenly home.

Last Thoughts on Transitions

Let me close our look at this fourth element of LifeMapping with a couple of parting suggestions. First, as much as God allows, anticipate transitions.

I have a friend who was in the defense industry and lives in Southern California. At one point, he looked around and realized a change was coming; new defense contracts would not keep rolling in steadily. And with the world changing, his job security was becoming as unsettled as the tectonic plates beneath Los Angeles.

That's when he began thinking in earnest about a second career. Not that he wanted to make a change, nor that one was imminent. But as they teach you in the Marine Corps, when the tactical situation gets bad, you never retreat. You just advance to a fallback position to continue the fight.

Just for fun, my friend took several aptitude tests and discovered that he had some artistic talent. As an engineer, he had used those abilities to create circuit boards and information pathways. Now he began taking art lessons as a hobby to develop his talent.

Before long, his hobby grew into displaying his work at small art fairs. Then he had a small show that highlighted his pewter and bronze works. Next, he storyboarded what it would take to start an art studio, involving his wife in the process.

By doing this contingency planning, they got a realistic look at where they would have to cut and what they could do if he lost his job one day (or simply decided to switch careers). Soon they began making financial sacrifices (including accelerating the payment of their mortgage) to put themselves in a position to be free to move in whatever future direction God had for them.

Seven years later, my friend did lose his job but not his bearings. By preparing well in advance for a "second season" career, he and his wife were ready to get back in the game when many of his unprepared friends were still scrambling to find a new playing field.

Take time to look down the road five years and, should the Lord tarry, anticipate the transitions looming ahead. Doing so can be a great help when the gate opens and change is fast upon you.

Second, don't be afraid to take that next step. One of my favorite verses that I've read and reread during times of transition is Joshua 1:9: "Have I not commanded you? Be strong and courageous! Do not be terrified nor dismayed, for the LORD your God is with you wherever you go."

Joshua was getting ready to take the reins of Israel's leadership from Moses and guide the people in a new, challenging direction. But he didn't make that transition alone. He had a mighty God who loved him and would be with him every step of the way.

Tim Burke, a wonderful person and friend, told his story in a book called *Major League Dad*. He loved his spouse and children enough to give up a Major League Baseball career to spend time with them. The world knows him as an All-Star pitcher who could have been making millions instead of staying home with kids with special needs.

I had the chance to see Tim at a pro athletes' conference here in Phoenix several years ago. And while Tim and I had the opportunity to talk only for a moment, I asked another active ballplayer how Tim was doing with the transition. He had heard someone ask Tim if he missed baseball, especially with spring training about to begin. "You bet I miss it," Tim said, and then with a smile he added, "and I've never been happier."

That's making a transition well. Not easily. Not without cost. But in a God-honoring way that moves him forward.

That's facing a major transition like Joseph and like the Lord Jesus.

Transitions aren't easy, and questions will come when you go through them. You bet I miss my grandparents and not having another chance to make things right with my father. You bet I'd turn back the clock if I could and take the lines of age and pain off my mother's face. You bet I miss hearing someone on the Today's Family team say, "Let's go get a yogurt," instead of going by myself.

But I've never been happier. And I pray the same for you.

The Next Step in the LifeMapping Process

We've taken a good deal of time looking at the past—looking at your strengths, freeze points, flash points, and untied transitions. Now it's time to follow your LifeMap to a place where there are no footprints. It's the future, and we'll look at four things you can do in seeking to make it a truly better place.

Digging Deeper

1. Describe in your own words how an untied transition differs from a flash point.

2. Dr. Trent uses the example of Joshua to illustrate what a transition is like. Read Joshua 1:1-11, 16-18. Describe the transition Joshua went through. What helped him face that transition successfully?

3. Dr. Trent talks about anticipating transitions. What major transitions can you expect to face in the next five to ten years? How can you prepare for them?

PART 3

...to Your Future

CHAPTER 9

Image Management vs. Authentic Living

IN OUR PREVIEW of the eight LifeMapping elements, we mentioned that after drawing out your strengths and struggles from the past, you now face an inescapable Y in the road. Whether you've realized it or not, the way you deal with your strengths and successes, freeze points, flash points, and untied or well-handled transitions comes down to two roads you can take toward the future.

If you take the high road, you're bound for *authentic living*. That's a road where you're able to look at your past honestly, learn from it, celebrate the positive things, grieve over parts of it if needed, but then move on in a healthy way. It's a road that has to be chosen each day, but you can be confident you're on it if you're practicing three important lifestyle traits I'll describe in this chapter.

The other road is taken all too often. In fact, it has become a common Christian choice. It's a road I call *image management*, and while it was prevalent in the early church, it's *epidemic* in ours today and rampant in the culture around it, especially in online sites like Instagram and in dating apps. It lures people by offering an imaginary way to live two lives, but it leaves you split off from yourself. It can be deadly to your relationships and to a healthy, fulfilling spiritual life.

What exactly do I mean by *image management* and *authentic living*, and how can you capture this area on your LifeMap? Let's answer those questions by looking first at an example of image management and the shimmering, deadly mirage it creates.

When Close Friends Go South

Have you ever found a kindred spirit who, from the first moment you met, bonded with you like a lifelong friend? That's what happened to Joan when she met a woman, Sara, who was to become one of her closest friends. Joan looked up to and greatly appreciated Sara. Unfortunately, Sara became one of the greatest examples of image management I've ever heard about.

Joan and Sara met at church, and from the beginning, everything clicked. They discovered they both liked to read mysteries. They had grown up in towns only twenty miles apart, and their high schools enjoyed a friendly if heated athletic rivalry. Now both women were avid tennis players.

As they began to peel back deeper levels toward a real friendship, they learned that each of them had come from a home with an abusive father. Both were active in the church, and Sara was even a Bible teacher in the women's fellowship. Joan would sit spellbound as Sara taught. Joan had never gone to church until after college. Listening to the way Sara communicated and clarified even those difficult parts of Scripture with such insight and confidence made Joan really want to step up her game in knowing and loving Jesus.

As the months went by, the two women spent more and more time together. They shopped, played tennis, and lunched as a team. They and their husbands went camping several times a year. Sara became a special friend and a mentor to Joan. But all that time, Joan didn't realize she was dealing with twins.

Sara didn't have a real identical sister. Think more like twins who are closely related but can think and act worlds apart. That's because Sara was immersed in image management. And over time, even the smartest, best image managers are headed toward a colossal collapse—like those pictures you've seen of a condemned structure collapsing inwardly and coming down in a moment when dynamited.

> Over time, even the smartest, best image managers are headed toward a colossal collapse.

Let me give you a definition of *image management* before you see it fleshed out in Sara's life.

Image management is the attempt to support a public self without dealing with private issues, which leads to increasing inner tension and, finally, a breakdown of values that will come to light, often in tragic ways.

You could say that that's just a hundred-dollar definition of *hypocrisy*. In Scripture, *hypocrisy* is a word that has to do with acting. But while actors (the good ones) seem to immerse themselves in a part, image management isn't acting. And actors don't (if they're emotionally healthy) go home and keep up their facade.

Rather, this is something else. In the vast majority of cases we've seen, image managers have suffered a serious hurt, often when they were young. But instead of dealing with it, they try to wrap a layer on the outside that works or looks great. Yet the more they choose to have one lifestyle that others see while ignoring the smoldering fire of a second, private life, the sooner the inner tension will spell doom for that public image.

Why? People tend to live out what they really believe about themselves. Let's say, for example, that in a clinical study a man looks at himself as a two on a one-to-ten scale. But then he's given a significant promotion. Yet he still feels, deep inside, like a two. Would that person tend to do well or poorly in the new position?

The answer is that initially, he'll tend to step up and do much better. But then, like skiers who hit a speed that puts them over their skis, he may crash and burn. It's almost as if the person is proving to himself and others that he really is a two, not a ten. And that's just in a workplace setting.

Joan will never forget the day she got the call from another church friend. Joan knew that other women made serious mistakes. She, from a broken background and years spent living out that hurt, knew she was fallen and flawed. But that would never happen with Sara. Yet the news was confirmed in the next morning's newspaper: Sara had embezzled thousands of dollars over a period of five years from the bank where she worked. She had also almost succeeded in framing an innocent coworker for the crime. And there was more.

There was that relationship with someone, not her husband, that had been hidden. And she was the epitome of the old lawyers' saying: "If there's one, there may or may not be two. But if there's two, there's twenty." There were far more than two as things came out. For those looking on, it was like that building that slowly shakes at first, but then the collapse seems to pick up speed as it crashes down. Consequently, Sara lost her job, her ministry post, a fifteen-year marriage, and by her choice, custody of her children.

Joan was crushed. Of all the Christian women she had met, Sara was the last one she would have ever expected to dishonor Jesus. But now Sara faced the likelihood of going to prison.

What happened in Sara's life and in the lives of many people like her? She had thrown all her efforts into building a public self. She put massive energy into creating an image, in this case a spiritual one. She wasn't just a nominal Christian; she appeared to be sold out. But it was only looks. The whole time, she had been pulling bricks out of the foundation of her life by refusing to honestly face problems in her private world. In fact, she never talked about them with anyone.

That's the problem with not facing the past—it's often a sure way of repeating it. Sara began supporting an image, not living authentically. And by trying to keep two worlds separate, she ended up increasing the internal pressure of a duplicitous life until all the joy and spark were gone and only image management was left—the last thing before the fall.

"But that's just one woman's story," you might protest. "That doesn't mean image management is footloose in the Christian community."

Really?

They Were Doing It All Right . . . Almost

If you think image management is practiced by only a select few, think again. Some people had it down pat in the first century.

Let's go back to Jesus' walking among those churches in the book of Revelation. To the church in Ephesus, John wrote:

> The One who holds the seven stars in His right hand, the One who walks among the seven golden lampstands, says this:
> "I know your deeds and your labor and perseverance, and that you cannot tolerate evil people, and you have put those who call themselves apostles to the test, and they are not, and you found them to be false; and you have perseverance and have endured on account of My name, and have not become weary."
> REVELATION 2:1-3

Doesn't that sound like one squared-away group of believers? In fact, if you remember, the Lord Jesus Himself ("the One who holds the seven stars") commended them seven times for their diligent work. (The number seven, biblically, is the number of completion.) They were All-Pros at doing things right—and at doing all the right things. But in the midst of all their doing, they left one thing out.

"But I have this against you, that you have left your first love" (Revelation 2:4).

They'd nailed it when it came to their image. But it was effort independent of honesty. They kept the outside of the cup shiny clean and left the inside full of rot. And it's still an incredibly common Christian choice today.

How easy it is to do all the right things! Spend time with the kids. Take them to Awana or the local youth program each week. Participate in a Sunday school class as well as church. Host a home fellowship. Be a part of visitation on Wednesday nights and the new members' class on Sunday afternoons. And add choir, MOPS, and Bible Study Fellowship just for good measure.

Do, do, do. And yet in all the doing of good, there's danger. Seriously. For effort without a right attitude can lead to callousness. And once you begin going through the motions, you're inching closer to simply maintaining an image.

What's the antidote?

What we've been talking about for chapters. Not wallpapering over those stories, positive and negative, that are a real and important part of your past but looking at your life authentically—in a way that sees and deals with and explores and grieves and repents of and moves past those tough things and poor decisions. It's making a choice to live without just looking in the mirror and walking away unchanged. It's making a choice for authentic living.

Recall Jesus' challenge to that group of Ephesian doers: "Remember from where you have fallen, and repent, and do the deeds you did at first; or else I am coming to you and I will remove your lampstand from its place—unless you repent" (Revelation 2:5).

Think of the powerful three-point sermon we saw earlier in that single verse. First, "remember from where you have fallen." Think back. Spend time in reflection. Look at the positive, but be honest about those seasons of hurt and open loops that are also a part of your past—like what you've been asked to do in the first four elements of LifeMapping.

Being authentic in dealing with your successes and failures involves taking an honest look back. And I can't think of a better tool to help you do that than LifeMapping, especially when done with a humble, contrite heart that's willing to repent and turn around if needed.

What a shock to find out that Sara's father, whom she never talked about or dealt with, had done many of the same things she'd done before he left the family when she was young! But that doesn't mean Sara was doomed or destined to act out the hurt or the example of brokenness that her father had given her. Because there is, in Jesus, a way of escape. It's the way found by the people we've already talked about who should have lived out broken lives of their own but didn't.

The second way out of image management is to "repent." Quit going through the motions and kidding yourself that you can have public and private selves that don't match up. Genuine repentance involves exchanging one way of life for another.

Then there's point three: "Do the deeds you did at first." Go back to basics. Get a clear, authentic plan for the future. As you'll soon see, that's exactly what you'll be doing in the final four elements of LifeMapping.

That leads to one more important thought from Jesus' encounter with the Ephesians. Jesus spoke to that church about an "or else." He was laying a choice before these people. They could head toward wholeness, health, humility, love, and life—what I'm calling authentic living. Or they could choose image management, where you try to be two people and you're in danger of losing that light Jesus puts in your life: "Or else I am coming to you and I will remove your lampstand from its place" (Revelation 2:5).

Like someone who has been stretching an extension cord until it's ready to pull out of the socket, if you don't turn around and begin walking in faith, you'll finally pull so far away from His strength that you lose your ability to shine God's light—and whatever position He's given you from which to share it.

Those are challenging thoughts. But know this: I believe we all, me included, choose to be image managers to some degree. We open the door and give a smile to our friend who shows up right in the middle of our yelling at our child who has accidentally broken a glass. We have a terrible day, and that perky waitress walks up and says, "So, how're you doing?" And we say great when we're anything but.

It's perfectly fine not to unpack our terrible day with the waitress. She's just being polite and welcoming. And it's okay to smile at that friend who shows up when we're still angry about an unresolved situation. But a true friend will see what's real on our face. And know this as well: So, too, do our children.

The first ones who see us being image managers instead of the real deal are our kids. They're like God's little spies. You can say anything you want. Have any number of verses on your walls. Have blog or podcast followers who think you're perfect. But your kids see reality. They may not understand it deeply at the time, but they see whether your faith, the life you're projecting, is the same at Home Depot or at church or with the neighbors outside—and at home when the doors are shut.

The goal of LifeMapping and authentic living isn't

perfection. Trying to be perfect leads to exhaustion and legalism and destroys freedom. Trying to convey an image of perfection leads to covering up all that hurt from the past, which leads to more hiding and duplicity and right into image management.

We'll look more closely at examples of image managers in a moment, but please know this: No matter your background, you have a choice to do something that is, in fact, the game changer of all game changers. Even if every toss of the coin, every option, is stacked against you, you can change the path you've been on. You can even change your father (or mother) if you need to.

"His Father David"

It might seem, at first glance, that there's an error in Scripture. That "error" is in 2 Kings 22. There we read, "Josiah was eight years old when he became king. . . . He did what was right in the sight of the LORD and walked entirely in the way of his father David" (2 Kings 22:1-2).

That all seems perfectly fine, but turn back just one chapter. There you'll discover more about Josiah, one of the youngest kings of Israel who had just ascended to the throne.

His grandfather Manasseh had been king before him for fifty-five years. And his grandfather was about the most wicked, horrible, child-sacrificing, divination-embracing, God-dishonoring king in all of Israel's history. And as wicked as he was in life, he also made sure that when he died, that terrible legacy would be remembered. He did that by being buried in a garden, not a cemetery—a garden right in the middle of his home where his son Amon and his grandson Josiah lived.

Think about that. If you're Josiah, every day you're walking by the grave of your grandfather, who was a terrible, horrible person. That memory of who he was is always there. That path he walked is inescapable.

And then, going back to chapter 21, after Manasseh's death, you meet Josiah's father, Amon. Amon, if it was possible, was even worse than his father! He was so bad, and hung around so many terrible people, that some of them decided to kill him (the literal Hebrew word means "slaughter") right "in his own house" (2 Kings 21:3) And guess where Amon was buried? Next to Manasseh, in the same garden in the house where Josiah lived.

Think of Josiah's background. A horrible, murdering grandfather. A father who was murdered in his own home. Both of them now buried right there. Always right there, reminding Josiah every day of who they were and of the path he seemed destined to take. And then, at eight years old, Josiah became king.

Which takes us back to that "error" in the Bible. There we're told: "Josiah was eight years old when he became king. . . . He did what was right in the sight of the LORD and walked entirely in the way of his father David" (2 Kings 22:1-2).

There it is again, what looks like error in Scripture! After all, we know his biological father was Amon, son of Manasseh, not David.

But what had Josiah decided to do?

He'd chosen the same thing that Joan, Sara's friend,

decided to do. He'd chosen not to follow what culture and so much of what passes for social science says is inevitable if you're from a crummy or even terrible background: He'd decided to switch fathers.

Josiah wasn't perfect, but even at eight years old, he knew that with God's love and power, he had a choice. With God's help and strength, he chose to walk in authenticity and light and love for God's Word—and in love for others. He chose a different father and a different king to follow. And Josiah's epitaph says he was one of the best kings Israel ever had.

It's hard to deal with a background that's dark or full of abuse or bad examples. But we don't have to ignore the hurt and try to live out a self-protective facade of a life. Rather, we can choose authentic living. We can be open to friends about our strengths and our failures. We can get counseling if we need it. We can work hard at this tool called LifeMapping. We can commit to being, as much as possible, the same person when we're alone with our families as we are at church or at work or in the community. And we

We can commit to being, as much as possible, the same person when we're alone with our families as we are at church or at work or in the community.

can repent and turn around and ask God and our loved ones for forgiveness when we make a mistake. "That's not who I want to be. I'm sorry. I want to be more like Jesus, and I'm sorry I got mad for what was an accident. Will you forgive me?"

That's where you want to go—living authentically. Capturing in your LifeMap just what you've done, over time, to move away from a hurtful past and toward a new direction in Jesus.

Still not sure what it means to be an image manager or to

choose authentic living? Let's get one more clear look at the deceptive trail image management presents, and then we'll add more to being authentic. Glance at the five questions below and see if they look like lifestyle choices you're making consistently. If they do, you're walking down that same road as Sara . . . and like an errant king named Saul.

Five Marks of an Image Manager

In the Old Testament, King Saul is a tragic figure. He was tall, dark, and handsome. He was also chosen by God when a stubborn people begged for a human ruler. But if Sara was a *practitioner* of image management, King Saul was a *grand champion*. Without a doubt, he would have had to answer yes to all five of the following questions. See if you would.

Are you great at beginning spiritual commitments but lousy at finishing them?

Saul was. In 1 Samuel 11:6 we read, "Then the Spirit of God rushed upon Saul." In the Old Testament, the Holy Spirit didn't reside on just anyone. At that time, the veil between God and humankind hadn't been ripped apart by Jesus' death, nor had Pentecost happened, which was when God the Holy Spirit came and indwelled each believer. Things were different for those living in Old Testament times. You can count on one hand the number of people God's Spirit "rushed upon" in that era, and it might surprise you to read that Saul was one of them.

Saul started with God's Spirit upon him. But he ended up seated in the slums by a witch, asking for her guidance. Later in 1 Samuel, we read, "The LORD did not answer him [Saul].

. . . Then Saul said to his servants, 'Find for me a woman who is a medium, so that I may go to her and inquire of her'" (1 Samuel 28:6-7).

God allows even great saints to walk away from His Spirit. It happened to Saul. It happened to Sara. They were fast starters but fifty-yard-dash runners in the marathon of life.

How about you? Are you a great starter and a poor finisher of spiritual commitments?

Does the fear of losing others' approval "force" you into increased compromise?

Image managers begin fighting desperately at times to keep one thing intact—not their integrity but their image. (Sound uncomfortably like any political figures in our day who we find out have two lives going?)

When Saul saw his image with the people going south, and a mighty army coming down from the north to battle him, he rushed into a compromising position.

We read, "Now he waited for seven days, until the appointed time that Samuel had set, but Samuel did not come to Gilgal; and the people were scattering from him. So Saul said, 'Bring me the burnt offering and the peace offerings.' And he offered the burnt offering" (1 Samuel 13:8-9).

If your image is at stake, who cares if sacrifices are only for priests to conduct? If compromising is what it takes to keep your followers on board, the ends justify the means, don't they? They do if you're Saul. But just as he finished doing what he thought he needed to do to protect his image, he saw Samuel walking up.

What was Saul's excuse when Samuel confronted him?

"Since I saw that the people were scattering from me, and that you did not come at the appointed time" (1 Samuel 13:11).

In other words, "It's your fault I did this, Samuel!"

Saul continued, "So I worked up the courage and offered the burnt offering" (1 Samuel 13:12). It's as if he's saying, "For the people, Samuel, not for me."

Really? That excuse didn't fly with Samuel, and it doesn't work for modern image managers either. They may cut corners in everything from drinking and sex to ethics in business to keep in place their "in-crowd" status or facade or clicks or likes, but it's all about image, and it's storing up judgment.

Does your fabricated image become more "real" than reality?

Saul simply didn't get that staying between the lines was for him. For other people maybe, but not for him. You see that in 1 Samuel 15, where God gave him a specific, if terrible, order. He was to be the instrument of divine judgment and eliminate an entire tribe. Amalek was to be destroyed, and along with him all his cattle and sheep, plus every one of his people, young and old.

But Saul let Amalek and the best of his livestock live, and he saved much of the spoils as well. What happened when Samuel confronted Saul over his disobedience?

"Saul said to him [Samuel], 'Blessed are you of the LORD! I have carried out the command of the LORD.' But Samuel said, 'What then is this bleating of the sheep in my ears, and the bellowing of the oxen which I hear?'" (1 Samuel 15:13-14).

And Saul's classic, image-driven response: "I *did* obey the voice of the LORD" (1 Samuel 15:20, emphasis added).

There's no objective reality with image managers. Truth

is what they need it to be, not the actual truth. They can become so good at being self-centered and deceptive that even doing something dead wrong can be grounds for celebrating how they've done something right.

Remember in our first chapter the story of Mary, whose husband walked away from her and refused any kind of counsel or reconciliation? He was totally convinced that even though God hates divorce and there were no grounds for his doing so, he was totally justified in walking away. He just switched churches, and soon relationships, without a blink. It wasn't his fault. Those words of warning or guidance didn't matter for him. It was her problem, not his. And he just knew that even if there was a problem with what he'd done, there is no judgment or consequence or unforgivable thing anyway.

I'm talking about the kind of person who would steal your car and run it into a light pole—but walk away praising the Lord that he wasn't scratched a bit though the car was totaled. "What was that pole doing there anyway?" he might say. "And why were your brakes so bad?"

Does your repentance involve sorrow about getting caught rather than sorrow about the act itself?

Several times we see where Saul was caught in a lie or bad behavior and corrected. But his repentance was always skin deep (and that's giving him a few folds). If you kick yourself for getting caught instead of mourning the loss of character involved or whom you might have hurt, you may be practicing image management. Particularly if you answer yes to the last question.

Do you refuse the counsel of others or the chance to change?

Saul brushed off correction from God's prophet. He wouldn't listen to his son Jonathan, either, when Saul strayed into sin by attacking David. He wouldn't listen to anyone who spoke God's Word . . . but he did ask to speak to that witch.

If you find yourself increasingly defensive or moving away from spiritual correction or godly counsel, watch out. That may be an attempt to prop up an empty image rather than hear God's clear direction through the advice and prompting of others.

And let me make something clear. I'm not saying counseling is the answer to everything, nor that all counselors are tremendously helpful. But when you refuse clear instruction like "Where there is no guidance the people fall, but in an abundance of counselors there is victory" (Proverbs 11:14), well, Houston, we have a problem.

The Antidote to Image Management: Authentic Living

The healthy, God-honoring approach to life is what I call authentic living. So how do you implement this choice? By adopting three lifestyle characteristics, each working together, that will develop authentic living and give you the strongest possible defense against image management.

Exercise the strength it takes to be humble.

First Peter 5:5 says, "God is opposed to the proud, but He gives grace to the humble." You could always tell when Saul was around. But you couldn't tell him much. There was the time he gave a foolish order for his troops to take no nourishment on the field of battle and thus robbed God's people of a great victory. When his son and soldiers urged him to change his orders, he would have put Jonathan to death to maintain his right to be wrong if his troops hadn't intervened (see 1 Samuel 14:24-46).

If you're a person who's used to going first class, it can be easy to build up an arrogance that says, "I've got an image. You'd better recognize it and cater to it."

It's like the stuffy British waiter who was obviously unimpressed by the dignitary seated at his table. After this "important" man had endured what he felt was inattention and inferior service for his station in life, he called the waiter over and said, "See here, sir, do you know who I am?"

"No, sir," said the waiter coldly. "But I shall make inquiries and inform you directly."

If you're allowing pride in your talents, person, possessions, or position to creep in, you're walking toward image management. Humility can put you back on the right road, the one the Lord Jesus took. He held the power to calm the sea and raise the dead, but "as He already existed in the form of God . . . [He] emptied Himself . . . [and] humbled Himself by becoming obedient to the point of death: death on a cross" (Philippians 2:6-8).

Commit to a life of continual learning.

I remember one professor in my doctoral program who took the word *attitude* and pushed it about two miles to the extreme. What an incredible chip on his shoulder! He was convinced that since he had his PhD, he was as close to being a god as you could get.

One way he demonstrated this was to require an incredible amount of reading from students. But I'll never forget someone asking him one day, in all seriousness, "Sir, what books have you read recently that you've benefited from?"

He replied haughtily, "I haven't read a book since graduate school, and I won't. My own research and understanding are better than anything in print."

Not only was that a lack of humility, but it also displayed an attitude that says, "I've stopped learning. I've got it. That's all I need." And it's a sure way to begin having to defend your positions rather than expand your horizons. Keep reading. Keep attending classes or workshops regularly. Keep going to church and sitting under others, especially if you think you know it all. Be willing to learn; be teachable. It's a great way to keep the "little gray cells" from melting down, and it's a powerful hedge against letting image management creep up on you.

Finally, be willing to build your own accountability base.

I won't go into detail on accountability here because it's a key part of the next chapter. But I'm convinced that accountability is at the heart of authentic relationships.

If you want to avoid image management, it's crucial to build your own accountability group. Such groups can provide relationships that hold untold riches, but they're a lot like buried treasure. You have to actively seek them out; they don't usually dig themselves up and drop right into your lap.

Humility, teachability, and accountability. Those three lifestyle choices will help you avoid image management and keep going right down the middle of the road marked *authentic living*.

Looking Over Your LifeMap

Take time now to go back over your LifeMap. Can you see a pattern or specific examples of when you chose image management? And even more important, can you see steps you've taken toward authentic living? Here's that part of my LifeMap that I displayed earlier, showing both.

For years in high school and on into college, I was so self-conscious and insecure about appearing weak that I did anything and everything I could that was hard: football, wrestling, pole vaulting, baseball. Even in noncontact activities like music, I had to do something challenging. I couldn't play just any instrument.

In eighth grade, I asked my music teacher what was the hardest instrument to play. Without hesitation, he said, "The bagpipes." That did it. I just had to take pipe lessons, and within three weeks I started. (What a mom!) After a year of instruction, and for the next five years, I played in the Phoenix Scottish Pipe Band. (I still drag out my pipes occasionally and play "Highland Laddie" or "Amazing Grace" just to watch Cindy, the girls, and Buddie the dog run for cover!)

"Doing everything the hard way" and "not wanting to intrude on anyone" might look laudable on the surface. But refusing to ask for or accept help was linked to an image I was keeping up, not authentic living. It wasn't until I had to ask for help in college (in particular, one time when I became extremely ill, had no money, and had to rely on someone else to pick me up and pay for me to go to a doctor) that I let go of an image-driven weakness.

On the other side of the coin, my learning to appreciate

John Trent's LIFEMAP

**IMAGE MANAGEMENT
VS.
AUTHENTIC LIVING**

↓

Wouldn't accept
help for years
Learning to lean
on others

Safety in
servanthood
Only the wise
seek counsel

Saw spouse's
strengths as God's
flashlight

Face west to
maintain humility

Cindy's detail strengths has been a great help to our marriage. Starting several years ago, Cindy and I made the decision to see an outstanding Christian counselor for three sessions every year as an enrichment experience. The first year, I remember our counselor, Dr. Bill Retts, asking, "So, what brings you two in?"

I answered, "Nothing! I'm sure you'll refund our money on the next two sessions after this morning."

But then Cindy pulled out her list!

While we could probably stand to go six times per year even today, the bottom line is that I'll still die long before I run out of issues to talk and learn about!

As for "facing west to maintain humility," that's a reference to something I've done for years to keep achievements in perspective. In my early Christian walk, when I was tempted to pride over some ministry or personal accomplishment, all I had to do was face west toward Phoenix (where I grew up) and think back to my non-Christian past. (During those years, I always lived east of Phoenix.)

I didn't come to Jesus until late in high school, and I had lived a less-than-honoring lifestyle before that time. In the Scriptures, Paul confessed that at times, he felt like "the least of the apostles" as he thought back to his time persecuting Christians (see 1 Corinthians 15:9). In the same way, "facing west" mentally helped keep me humble and make me thankful that God could forgive and use me in spite of my past.

You say you're committed to walking the road of authentic living? Great. Then it's time to turn the page and take another step in the right direction—namely, the sixth step in the LifeMapping process: storyboarding clear goals and directions for your most important relationships. In the next chapter, you'll turn your storyboarding skills loose on a positive plan for your future.

Digging Deeper

1. How would you summarize the difference between image management and authentic living?

2. Dr. Trent refers to Revelation 2:5 in this chapter. After rereading that verse, describe the three steps for getting out of image management. (Remember. Repent. Do the deeds you did at first.) What do those things mean for you personally? What, for you, are "the deeds you did at first"?

3. If you haven't already done so, fill out the image management versus authentic living part of your LifeMap.

4. In which one area (or with which group of people) are you most tempted to work on your image rather than your integrity? Why do you think that is?

CHAPTER 10

Gaining a Clear Life Plan

HAVE YOU EVER planned something and had it turn out much differently from what you expected? That's exactly what happened to me with some special plans I made for Cindy on our first wedding anniversary. It was 1980, and our paper anniversary was coming up soon. Like any sensitive husband, I easily remembered our wedding date. (Thankfully, right on our kitchen table was a silver serving plate with the date on it to remind me every day.)

But what was I to do to make that first anniversary special?

We were living in Dallas at the time, and I was a youth pastor at a fine church, making all that great money. Actually, we were so broke. But a good friend mentioned a wonderful restaurant he'd dined at, one I'd heard about but had never been to. It was the Petroleum Club in downtown Dallas, high atop the Southland Life Building.

The more he talked, the more this sounded like just the place for our first anniversary. Then I asked him about the prices . . . and when he told me, I sounded as if they'd just turned off my iron lung.

Crestfallen, I headed back to work, trying to scale down my dinner plans from high atop the Southland Life Building to underneath the Golden Arches. Then suddenly an idea hit me. No . . . but yes. It could work! It *would* work! There was one place we had stashed away some money for something that really wasn't that big a deal.

I called my friend, who helped arrange everything for me. He got a friend who was a member of the Petroleum Club to sponsor me for dinner that night, and my surprise plans were beginning to take shape!

All I told Cindy about the evening was that we were going "somewhere incredibly special" and that she needed to wear something just a fraction less fancy than her wedding dress.

We drove downtown, got in the glass elevator and goggled at the magnificent view, and then walked into a truly five-star restaurant. They treated us as if we owned the place. Throughout the experience, we had six waiters and helpers come by our table (five of whom we didn't really need). Our name had been beautifully engraved on a matchbook cover (which we still have). A strolling violinist roamed the aisles, and a photographer took our picture. (I was sure we'd end up on the society page.)

The food was exquisite. We sat at a window table enjoying the fantastic view. Here I was with a beautiful wife who loved me, and she was all decked out in a gorgeous dress. On our anniversary. I even had enough cash in my pocket to pay for everything, including the exorbitant tip and all the pictures I'd initially thought were free.

As we drove home, you can imagine the glow cast over the evening. Candlelight dinner . . . beautiful setting . . . celebrating our love and anniversary . . .

We had an old Maverick with a bench seat. And Cindy was laying her head on my shoulder as we drove home. No kids. First anniversary. Awesome evening. Was this going to be a romantic night or what?

Here's how it turned out to be "or what."

As we neared home, my loving, practical, detailed, organized wife purred, "Sweetheart, that was a wonderful dinner."

Sweetheart, I thought. *This is going to be a great evening.*

"But can I ask you something?" she said, almost whispering in my ear.

Ask me anything. I'm yours!

"Where did we get the money for that kind of dinner?"

Oh, no! Don't ask me that!

When a loving, practical, detailed, organized wife asks you a financial question, and then you pause instead of answer—you can imagine what happened next.

"Honey, where did you get the money?"

Honey. It's gone from Sweetheart *down to* Honey.

"Jooohhhnnn!"

Not John*!*

With a loving, practical, detailed, organized wife, it's never good to lie. As we pulled into our driveway, I turned to her, took her hands in mine, and said, "Honey, I don't know how to tell you this . . . but we just ate our couch."

The only extra money we had at the time was the money we'd been saving toward a couch. But there was plenty of time to put that money away again! After all, it was our anniversary. Not only that, but I had liberated that money from the low-percentage-rate account it had been languishing in and used it to help stimulate the Dallas economy.

"Honey, I don't know how to tell you this . . . but we just ate our couch."

Suffice it to say that none of those (and many other quickly-thought-up) explanations worked, and there was no "touchy the toes" that night!

Seriously, I'm thankful that God has given me a forgiving, loving, practical, detailed, organized wife who still loves me but still can't believe what I did that first anniversary, now more than forty years ago. (And believe me, I only did it once.)

That's a dramatic example of planning something and having it go all *wrong*. What I'd like to do in this chapter is to help you look at your life and lay out plans, goals, and ideas that can help things go *right*.

LifeMapping and Time Management

There are countless good books that can help you with the specific details of time management. Our goal in this chapter isn't to build a weekly calendar. Rather, it's to get an overall plan that can become both a prayer guide and the means to an action plan in those key areas of your life.

While many of your storyboard posts may ideally end up on a to-do list, think first of overall goals and then of how to move them into action. But how do you plan life goals?

Start by picking out the key roles in your life right now and putting each one on a topper card.

For example, let's say you're single, and as you look over your roles and responsibilities, your life plan headers look like this:

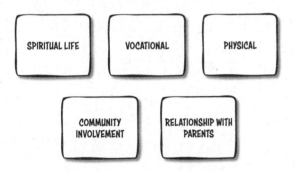

Whatever your toppers end up being to fit your particular situation, you use the same storyboarding technique you've used all along to fill out the subbers. And while you can get as detailed as you like, here are four questions that can help you flesh out the subber cards under each header:

1. What do I need to do in this area?
2. What do I want to do beyond the essentials?
3. How can I accomplish it?
4. Who am I encouraging to help keep me responsible for my goals?

With those four questions in mind, you can begin to fill in the subbers under each of your key personal and vocational roles, and you'll start to see a set of clear goals taking shape.

Key Categories for Goals

For the sake of illustration, the next page shows my LifeMap from when I still had children under my roof, with the edited goals I came up with in the major areas of my life. I used the toppers Spiritual Life, Marriage, Father, and Profession. You may come up with ten cards that help you flesh out this element of your LifeMap, or you may have only two or three. The important thing is to seek a personal balance in gaining a clear plan in at least three major areas: your spiritual life, your personal life, and your vocation.

Under my LifeMap, I first storyboarded the topper Spiritual Life. As I thought about the four leading questions above, I came up with the following abridged list.

Spiritual Life

"Read through the New Testament" means a daily plan of Bible reading that would take me through the New Testament twice in one year. This (along with prayers) answered the first question of what I needed to do to meet the basics of a growing spiritual life. Then, regarding the second question about things I'd like to do, I determined that reading an outstanding book on the life of Jesus (like those by my friends Max Lucado or Ken Gire) would be a positive goal. And finally, I listed "Look for opportunities to share Jesus" as a further goal for maintaining a missions outlook wherever I am, at home or away.

Once I'd storyboarded this first topper, I just went across the row of toppers, filling out the subbers under each. In the case of my goals and plans as a husband and father, I storyboarded this part with Cindy's input and encouragement.

John Trent's LIFEMAP

GAINING A CLEAR LIFE PLAN

SPIRITUAL LIFE
Read through NT
Read *Life of Christ* book
Look for opportunities to
share Jesus

MARRIAGE
Listening ear
Pray Scripture for wife
Maintain weekly date
night

FATHER
Accept emotions
Quality time
Pray Scripture for
daughters

PROFESSION
Live up to ministry name
Quality service and
responses

That way, I wasn't coming up with another "We ate the couch!" plan that sounded great to me but came far short of meeting her needs and reality.

Marriage

With Cindy, my goals were to maintain a listening ear (not a lecturing mouth), to take a section of Scripture and pray God's Word for her, to have regular dates with her to keep our relationship fresh, and to be accountable to the small group I was in through our church.

What I mean by praying God's Word for her is to take actual Scripture verses and personalize the passages by praying them specifically for Cindy. For example, "Lord, may You be my wife's shepherd. May You cause her to lie down in green pastures and give her rest this morning. May You guide her this day with Your rod and protect her with Your staff . . ." That's personalizing and praying Psalm 23 for her.

Several good books list many Scriptures already designed for you to personalize prayers based on the Scriptures for your loved ones, like the excellent *Praying God's Will for Your . . .* series of books by Lee Roberts. (There are volumes on praying for your wife, husband, son, or daughter.)[1]

Father

Then Cindy helped me flesh out my goals as a father. As you'll notice, that list began with "accept emotions," and there's a specific reason for it.

I grew up in a fairly unemotional home, with a mother who handled things calmly like the businesswoman she was and two brothers who were also pretty relaxed (except for the time my older brother accidentally shot me with a spear gun and things heated up pretty quickly).

It only seems logical, therefore, that out of that semi-calm, relatively quiet background, the Lord would give me a wife, two daughters, and even a hyperactive female dog to share my life with! And while Cindy doesn't lean too far on the emotional side of things, both Kari and Laura are a bouquet of varied emotions.

I can't say I've understood them all, or that I've always responded well to their laughter and tears followed by intense times of reflection and more laughter, more tears, and so on. But valuing them and their emotions is a major goal I have worked at to demonstrate my love.

Along with understanding and accepting their emotions, I've had to work at dealing with my own. For example, for a time, whenever I'd get really upset with the kids over something they had done (like being "too emotional"), I'd point my finger at them just to emphasize my displeasure.

"Why are you being so angry with the kids?" Cindy would ask.

I'd always come back with the line, "I'm not angry. I'm just being emphatic." (I made sure to never point at her when I was being emphatic!) Actually, I was frustrated, but I didn't recognize it as such.

Then Cindy came back with a piercing comment wrapped in a question: "Wasn't one of the cards on your LifeMap about listening and trying to understand my and the girls' feelings about things?"

Ouch. It didn't take me long to realize that she was right and that things needed to change. If I wanted that card to stay up and have any credibility, I needed to get out of the habit of pointing my finger at them—and recognize and deal with the emotions I had when I was frustrated.

So one evening, I called Kari and Laura into the living room and asked them to forgive me for the times when I'd gotten angry and pointed at them. "To show you I'm serious about this," I went on, "anytime from now on that Dad gets angry and points at you in anger, he will give you a one dollar bill on the spot."

Instantly you could see their eyes open wide. "A whole dollar?" Laura asked.

"Yes," I said.

And then for the next four weeks, both kids did their best to provoke me to point at them!

To my discredit, I was well on my way to funding their college education at Harvard after the first two weeks of making that pledge. While I didn't keep an exact account, I must have shelled out close to twenty dollars in pointing fees. But after that, I'll bet I didn't lose another dollar—except when Laura looked at me with those "melt your heart" brown eyes and said, "Dad, I'm so broke. Won't you just get upset and point at me?"

That change for me wasn't just because I got tired of reaching into my back pocket and emptying my wallet—though I have to admit that helped. Rather, I had that card on my LifeMap as the policeman, gently reminding me each time I looked at it that my kids are worth far more than any finger pointing. And besides, I wanted to have the credibility to leave that card on my LifeMap!

The other cards in my Father area included quality time (defined very differently for each girl) and, as with Cindy, praying Scripture for their safety and spiritual and physical growth. And once again, I made myself accountable in this area to my small group.

One last recommendation is a great book that helped me with understanding and dealing with emotions and attachment in marriage. It's called *Created for Connection* and was written by my good friend Kenneth Sanderfer, along with Dr. Sue Johnson, who founded EFT (Emotionally Focused Therapy).

Profession

Then, finally, the last topper card relates to my profession. While I've shown you the edited version of my LifeMap due to space limitations, two things remain prominently placed on my subber cards (besides making myself accountable once more).

First, I want to pursue the goal stated in the name of my ministry, StrongFamilies, when I'm talking and dealing with all people. Second, I want to build quality service and a response system that honors each person who attends a seminar or contacts my office by email or phone.

I can't say I've mastered this last card yet in beginning a ministry with a two-person staff of Kari, our older daughter, and me. Since I'm the shipping department one day, the counseling department the next, and the correspondence department on day three, I sometimes have to keep people waiting for a return email or phone call much longer than I'd like. But I'm working on this card.

In brief, then, by developing the subbers under those four topper cards, I came up with this abridged version of my LifeMap. I realize that your headers might look very different, and your list of subbers could easily be much longer underneath. But regardless, now is a great time to put down the book, head to your storyboard corner, and use brainstorming and sharpening to flesh out those key elements of your life.

Three Words to Guide Your Goal-Setting Process

As you do this part of your LifeMap, keep in mind the following three words. They will help you to create a plan that's realistic and practical.

Credibility

As you sit down individually or with your spouse or a small group to gain a clear life plan, it's important to commit yourself to credibility. One way to think of credibility is in two words you hear when you say this single word: *credit* and *ability*. In other words, *credibility* means that God and others can take your words and actions right to the bank. So if you put up a card like "Accept emotions" under your Father card as I did, you need to be willing to walk the walk, not just talk the talk. And you gain credibility by working consistently toward making what's on your cards a vital, everyday part of your life.

Confidence

You may not think of confidence as an important part of fleshing out a life plan, but it's actually vital. First of all, lean on Proverbs 3:26: "The LORD will be your confidence." If you take the time to carefully and prayerfully storyboard goals in each major area of your life—goals that honor Jesus and help you love Him and others more effectively—you can lean on Him for strength to make those plans a reality.

And also keep Hebrews 10:35-36 in mind: "Do not throw away your confidence, which has a great reward. For you have need of endurance, so that when you have done the will of God, you may receive what was promised."

Confidence in a God-honoring plan can also give you endurance to stay the course and keep moving forward—all the way to the promise of love, peace, and joy that comes from loving and serving Jesus. And finally, you'll see your confidence increase the more you base your life plan on the Word of God.

I've always been thankful for my four years at Dallas Theological Seminary, but I didn't realize until a few years ago one important side benefit of its intense instruction in the Scriptures (like requiring students to take both Hebrew and Greek, the original languages of the Old and New Testaments). What does learning God's Word have to do with confidence?

In a study done on the connection of prayer, attachment to God, and psychological well-being, one thing stood out loud and clear. Closeness to God leads to health and confidence.[2] And what promotes closeness to God better than getting to know Him through intense study of His Word?

You'll never go wrong if you tie your life plans into God's Word. It will give you a sense of mission, strength, and confidence that can keep you going during those times when you need endurance.

Communication

Credibility and confidence are good starters, but to pull off your life plan, you'll also need to communicate it to friends, family members, and any other people you can rely on to hold you accountable. In other words, don't be the kind of person who works out a life plan and then walks in the door and announces, "Honey, guess where we're moving tomorrow?"

If you're married, sitting down with your spouse to come up with a life plan as a couple is vital. Additionally, discussing it with others adds to the commitment and confidence to make it a reality.

Credibility, confidence, and communication centered on a clear plan—that's what you can think about now as you list the major areas of your life and then begin storyboarding positive details under each one. But without someone to hold you accountable when you're finished, your chances of seeing your plan come off your LifeMap and into real life decrease dramatically. Below are just a few reasons I believe loving accountability is so important, as mentioned in the last chapter.

Accountability: Helping Each Other Live Out Your Faith

In July 1993, I had the privilege, along with some 54,000 other men, to take part in the Promise Keepers national conference in Boulder, Colorado. Talk about incredibly inspiring! To sing "How Great Thou Art!" with 54,000 men, arm in arm and hearts knit together, seemed as close to a heavenly men's choir as I could experience until I actually arrive there.

Promise Keepers operates by a simple set of principles. Men need a relationship with their heavenly Father through our Lord Jesus Christ. And men need each other. But what does that require?

It's one thing to stand on a (almost literal) mountaintop in Colorado. It's another to live out your faith back home.

That's why the men I know who really lived out the changes they sang about did something incredibly powerful when they got home. They got into a small group.

Of course, the same is also true for women. They, too, need each other and need to hold one another accountable as sisters in Christ. A women's Bible study, a couples group with you and your spouse, or a group of girlfriends are places where you can build this kind of relationship.

I encourage you to go through your LifeMap with a small group of friends who are committed to you. When I first showed my LifeMap to the small group I was in, some things weren't easy to talk about. Those cards on your LifeMap can be very personal, and I'm not suggesting you pass them out at a movie theater to total strangers. But in the safe company of a supportive friend or group of people you know, trust, and love, showing your LifeMap can make your goals more real and tangible.

Final Thoughts on Life Planning and Goal Setting

Let me say again that this chapter and this element of the LifeMapping process aren't meant to take the place of some of the highly tuned time-management tools on the market. What we're after here is more of a broad brushstroke that can at least get you started in the planning process—and in setting up a target that you can ask God to help you hit. But there's one final application that I highly recommend. Namely, once you have your plan in place, sit down at least once a year for a time of review and refocusing.

With the flash points and transitions we've already talked about that spring up in our lives, your LifeMap may look very different a year from now. That's why it's important to be flexible and to consistently evaluate and fine-tune the process. At a minimum, link a yearly physical exam with your review of your LifeMap. That way, you've got a built-in reminder to check up on your physical, relational, and spiritual health.

For all of us, planning can be much different from putting something into practice. And in the seventh and eighth elements of LifeMapping that follow, you'll discover two crucial tools to help turn all your writing into reality.

The first is a key element called learned hopefulness. It can help you put away the natural tendency to fall back into negative patterns and past hurts. The second, called memorial markers, can give you tangible targets to help keep you moving toward that positive future you've just outlined.

Digging Deeper

1. In this chapter, Dr. Trent talks a lot about plans and goals. Read Proverbs 3:5-6. How would you summarize the essential attitude required for choosing the right goal, plan, or "path"? What do you think it means to "acknowledge" God when making plans?

2. If you haven't already done so, list each of the key roles you play in life on a topper card. Then on subber cards, write out simple, specific goals for each role.

3. Proverbs 27:17 talks about how one friend can help another. Read that verse and then pick a friend (it could be your spouse) with whom you can share the goals you wrote down above. Ask him or her to help you critique (or "sharpen") your goals.

4. After you've refined your goals with the help of your friend, write out specific steps you plan to take to achieve them. It may be helpful to attach deadlines to your tasks. Set a date for reviewing your life plan in one year.

CHAPTER 11

Learned Helplessness vs. Learned Hopefulness

As WE GET READY to talk about the seventh key element of LifeMapping, a concept called *learned hopefulness*, something may already be bothering you. You may now have a positive plan mapped out and prayed over. But could it come true in any real-life sense? What about all those other, ultimately unsuccessful times you set out to move in a more positive direction with your health, heart for God, or home? What makes this life-plan mapping any different?

It's Only a (True) Story

In creating your LifeMap, perhaps you've run into the harsh reality that your marriage, children, and work don't seem to fit neatly within a simple post. Perhaps your spouse isn't interested in helping you create your LifeMap—or in ever doing his or her own. And there seems little hope that will change anytime soon. So why not just put this plan back in a folder with all the others that haven't brought real improvement?

If that's your perspective on where you've come so far, you'll love this next aspect of LifeMapping. That's because it's all about a biblical method of facing the inevitable barriers that stand between any plan and positive change—and it's about how to move beyond them, in some cases for the first time.

With that in mind, let me introduce you to two concepts you'll soon become familiar with. One is a positive tool I want you to put into practice called *learned hopefulness*. The other is the dark side of that same concept, *learned helplessness*. We'll look at learned hopefulness first, and I'll start by illustrating it with the abbreviated story of my friend Dave Dravecky. He's been through a lifetime's worth of challenges and changes.

When Your LifeMap Seems to Fall Apart

It took only a split second on that cool August night in Montreal's Olympic Stadium. Sixty feet, six inches from home plate, Dave Dravecky's future snapped in the midst of a pitch. In the instant it took for his arm to break, all his comeback dreams, all his carefully laid plans, were shattered. With a *crack* that could be heard by those in the upper deck, a Cinderella story ended like a nightmare.[1]

In the weeks that followed, the decisions were agonizing; the prayers, real; the surgery, radical. And while the doctors assured him that the cancer was gone, so was his arm.

It wasn't just part of his arm, either, but the entire arm and most of his shoulder.

Dave had to take many difficult first steps following his surgery. The first time he forced himself to stand in front of the mirror and look at the hole where his arm had been. The first time he struggled to button his shirt with one hand. The first time he stared at his shoelaces and wondered how in the world he was going to tie them. And always there was the phantom pain that felt as if his fingertips were on fire when there were no fingers there to feel anything.

I had the privilege of dining with Dave and his exceptional wife, Jan, on the eve of another first for Dave. The next morning, he was to face a horde of eager television talk-show hosts and newspaper reporters who had descended on Orlando for his first public interview since the operation.

The interviews would go incredibly well. His words conveyed to millions of viewers a crystal-clear testimony of his undaunted courage and his unshakable faith in Jesus Christ. But the night before, at dinner, a group of us got to hear about an even more touching first . . . and indirectly learned a great deal about learned hopefulness.

Dave had taken facing live cameras and national media attention in stride in his years as a successful baseball star. Much more difficult for him was the prospect of how his two children would react to seeing him for the first time with no left arm.

The Day Daddy Came Home

Dave and Jan had decided not to have the kids come to the hospital during his short stay after the amputation. Instead, the day Dave came home, they brought each child into a room, one by one, to see Daddy.

Their son, Jonathan, was the first to come in. An energetic nine-year-old at the time who loved baseball and his father, he walked all around the room, looking at Dad from all angles without saying a word.

Finally, Dave said to him, "Well, do you want to see my scar?"

"Yeah!" Jonathan said, his eyes lighting up.

Carefully removing the bandages, Dave showed him the massive job of suturing that had been done on his shoulder.

"Wow, Dad!" Jonathan said. "Wait right here. Don't move a muscle. I'll be right back, I promise. Don't go anywhere."

Several minutes went by before Jonathan came back in the room and said, "Dad, I've got some of my friends outside. Can they come in and see your scar too?"

Any doubts Dave might have had about his son being distant or uncomfortable around him were dispelled as he became the best show and tell object on the block!

Young boys take scars as a badge of honor. But would the same thing happen with their daughter, Tiffany? Or would an empty sleeve put a barrier between the two of them?

Their precious daughter had waited patiently outside for her turn to see Daddy. When it finally came, she ran to him. And when she reached him, he was able to do something he hadn't done for weeks with his painful, cancerous arm in a sling—give her a big hug.

"Well, what do you think?" he asked with his irrepressible smile.

"Daddy," she said, "I'm glad they took your arm off."

"You are?" he asked, taken off guard. "How come?"

"Because now you can hug me again."

As traumatic as his experience was in many ways, Dave wasn't broken by what happened to him. Shaken, yes. Set back. Honest about his struggles. But not shattered.

He would never climb a mound again as a professional baseball pitcher, never again put his rally cap on in the dugout or get another strikeout to go in his record book. In an instant, his status as a pro pitcher dropped totally out of the box scores. But that didn't finish Dave Dravecky. It just moved him into a different league.

In the Official Scorer's Book of Life—the one that tracks each of us daily as a spouse, a parent, and a godly man or woman—Dave pitched a winning game. He may have switched positions from a ballplayer to a spectator, but as a person, he made it to the All-Star Game.

Only Two Choices

Like Dave Dravecky, you have only two choices when you face challenges to your neatly-laid-out LifeMap. Those two options are very different. And the choice you make will radically affect the way you treat others, how highly you value yourself, and even your personal health.

What are your options?

Dave Dravecky illustrates one choice you can make—to confidently and positively face the future. Again, it's what I call *learned hopefulness*.

What comes from the Dravecky school of facing the future? Try an honest optimism that leads to action, not denial. It spurs you to make a clear plan, keeps a tremendous, lifelong challenge before you, and draws out your best efforts at commitment and self-control.

The other choice of perspective is *learned helplessness*. I'll say more about it shortly.

When Life Sets Forth That Choice

The choice between the two approaches when our future is challenged is often launched by that day we realize a huge change is coming. Consider these examples.

- A sixty-four-year-old major airline captain suddenly realizes his scheduling supervisor is counting down the flights until he (the captain) is forced to retire. Where did all that time to prepare go? Now what?
- The rumor that a number of long-term employees are being laid off shoots through your department so fast that even an Iron Dome defense couldn't stop it.
- Your parents notify you that after graduation, your subsidized lifestyle is going to change radically, and there's no great job on the horizon.
- The ultrasound confirms that it's not just one kid coming in a few months but twins.

We can't avoid changes, either long expected or "Here they come!" We do, however, have a choice in how we respond.

When Your Prayed-Over Plan Is Challenged

In the last several chapters, you've been encouraged to look at the key areas of your life and map out (or storyboard) a plan for moving forward. But you may be facing a major challenge to one or more of your goals. While it may not be nearly as life-threatening as the cancer Dave Dravecky faced, it can be more than enough to stop any steps toward a positive future. So what can help you move forward?

Let's go on Christmas break and see what kept one couple's positive plan from being tossed aside.

It Still Can Be a Wonderful Life

Let's meet Angel and Bernita. While many people look at Christmas as the "most wonderful time of the year," it was the worst time for them and their children.

Both Angel and Bernita were first-generation Christians. They had worked hard at understanding their past. They'd experienced plenty of freeze points and flash points. And there were untied transitions because so little had changed in their parents' homes and lives. Both Angel and Bernita came from the same small town, and both came from dysfunctional, alcoholic, faith-mocking families.

However, they believed that in Jesus, they had everything they needed to choose a new direction for their family. So in creating their LifeMaps, they loved working through the strengths and struggles. Being challenged to choose authentic living over image management. And setting up positive plans for their marriage and, especially, parenting.

But then came Christmas.

It's true that there are vacations, and then there are trips back home. Every time Angel and Bernita went back home for Christmas, the clock would rewind until they were angry seventeen-year-olds again. There was still the drinking anytime day or night. The swearing. The dishonor that was a way of life. And the way their parents would watch things on television that no five- and seven-year-olds (the ages of their children) should ever see. And, as in their own childhoods, their parents didn't care.

It's true that there are vacations, and then there are trips back home.

It did no good to address this with their parents. That would just lead to verbal fights. And while their parents brushed off everything as no big deal, Angel and Bernita both felt they had just been sucked into a dance that they'd spent years trying to get away from. To ask their parents to respect their boundaries in how they raised their children brought only contempt. After all, it was their parents' home. Their rules.

So what do you do? Never go back?

It was important to protect the children and not be drawn into cycles of anger and hurt. But Angel and Bernita knew as well that staying away didn't change their relationship with their parents. It just put all those issues in an emotional freezer. At one point they went two Christmases without going home. But the next time they went back, it was as if everything had thawed out and things were just like the last time they'd walked out the door.

So, again, what do you do?

When You Plan in Hopefulness
Instead of Choosing Helplessness

Here's what Angel and Bernita did with a little coaching—something you can also do to protect your positive plan from the previous chapter and keep it from blowing up. Angel and

Bernita came up with a list of things that challenged all that hard work they'd done in building their positive plan. The first thing on their list?

Christmas.

So we started there. And they created a plan (or storyboard) to face the holidays in a different way.

They mapped out what, in their home, they'd like to do to celebrate the birth of Jesus. Looking at lights. Going with their small group and all their children to serenade those in a nursing home near their church.

But they also made a plan for that trip home and what could make it different from those they'd had before.

They decided to save up and pay to stay in a hotel. That way, if things got terrible, they could leave their parents' homes at any point without all the drama and emotion of packing up that they'd experienced in the past.

Then they'd pick several events outside their parents' homes that they'd build into the visit. But they'd invite each set of parents to join in. For example, they'd visit a Christmas tree farm and go to a Christmas carol service.

And they called in some help. They had several friends who had also navigated difficult trips back home, and Angel and Bernita asked them to add ideas to this part of their LifeMap. The friends loved seeing the LifeMap and sharing what had worked for them.

In short, Angel and Bernita looked at their plan and then took time to put up posts about what they could see coming toward them. They planned *in advance* for those areas they knew could blow up their plan.

You can't anticipate everything (such as walking into your office and finding everything from your desk tossed into two boxes with a final check and note saying you've been dismissed). But you can look at those key areas of your life and ask, *Lord, give me wisdom on what could blow up my plans for the future.*

And one more important thing: Know that you can't out-logic your emotions. Let me risk redundancy by repeating that: *You can't out-logic emotions.*

Here's what I mean: Many people beat themselves up emotionally, and some even give up on change being real, because they think that having a plan will erase not just barriers but also the emotions that come with them. Let me give you an example.

Think about being at a movie. They've just dimmed the lights, and the previews are running. Some people enter your row, Cokes and extra-large popcorn buckets in hand, trying to get back to their seats. They don't see you and accidentally step on your feet.

What's your first reaction when a grown man in a size-eleven shoe steps on your size-five foot? *Ouch!* The pain comes immediately. And (be honest here) what comes next 99.9 percent of the time?

The emotion. *That hurt! I'm mad! Why did you do that?* But as your emotion simmers and you feel the pain, the person with the Coke and popcorn is apologizing. Over and over, he says he's sorry. It's obvious he means it. And *then* logic kicks in and you tell him it's okay (even if your foot is still sore).

But do you see what came first? When you get hurt—or you see someone you love get hurt—your automatic reaction isn't something you can plan out of existence.

When Angel and Bernita are at home and someone speaks

a word in anger (as has happened so many times before), the hurtful words will pluck a string on an emotion that reverberates, reawakening hurt from the past. You can't out-logic that emotion of anger, shame, or hurt.

But what they—and you—can do is know (and even have it on the LifeMap) that someone will "step on your foot" when you go home for Christmas. Amazingly, just planning for the fact that it's going to be difficult helps to make it less so. It doesn't erase it. It doesn't keep it from happening. But just as you know that if it's Tuesday, it's Double Star day at Starbucks, so also if you go home for Christmas for any length of time, you're *going to* hear hurtful words.

I coach people like Angel and Bernita to picture themselves walking into a home like that with an invisible piece of plastic wrapped around them. And when those hurtful words come, they don't get through to the heart. They bounce off. And it's something you can get through, starting with a deep breath and a prayer.

That's when logic can kick in. Should we go? Or can we change the subject? But what we don't have to do is be caught up in that negative emotion that's coming. As Martin Luther was credited with saying, "You can't keep birds from flying over your head, but you can keep them from building a nest in your hair."[2]

You don't have to be perfect. No plan is perfect. But by choosing learned hopefulness (what we've just modeled) over learned helplessness (which we'll look at next), you don't have to beat yourself down for being human. You don't have to fail at having a non-angry, non-drama-filled homecoming when it hasn't happened in fifteen years.

So come up with as many posts and potential examples as

you can that are like Christmas for Angel and Bernita. What do you know is likely to impede your plan for growth and life? What can you do now to handle it when it happens?

But this is also where we look at the opposite of learned hopefulness, *learned helplessness.*

What Is Learned Helplessness?

Remember when Moses led the people of Israel out of Egypt? They'd been in bondage for four hundred years. It's what they knew, as terrible as it was. And guess what the people did when things got really tough in their journey through the desert to the Promised Land? They cried out to Moses, "Let's go back to Egypt!"

Learned helplessness is feeling that there's nothing you can do to get where you so much want to go—most often because of things that have happened in your past. Your history of negative experiences has you convinced that you may as well go back to dysfunction or bondage because there is no way forward. Let's look at some examples of that kind of thinking.

What Can Push Us to Practice Learned Helplessness

I'm thirty-four years old, and I've been married three times. (Dr. Trent, it's not my fault; I always seem to pick losers.) My problem is my hair . . . or lack of it.

I know that many men feel there's nothing wrong with being bald, but I do. I started losing my hair when I was in high school, and I've tried everything

I know since then to stop what's happening to me or to reverse it.

I know that my first wife left me because of my hair. My latest wife even told me straight out that I was obsessed with my hair and that was why she was leaving.

My lack of hair is ruining my life. I know it's the reason I'm not making sales like I used to. I can tell that people just look at me differently.

When I was eighteen, I had hair implants put in, and then again at twenty-one. I even went to a well-known plastic surgeon recently and offered to pay him in advance for transplanting whatever skin I needed to fix my head.

All he did was insult me by saying that I shouldn't waste my money on scalp surgery—the money I spent on my head should go into seeing a psychiatrist!

I'm sure that doctor wasn't a Christian. That's why I'm writing you to ask your advice.

That was a letter I received from someone that illustrates, albeit in a dramatic and unhealthy way, one thing that causes us to choose to be helpless and unable to change.

We choose helplessness when the key to change is in the past.

When it comes to facing the future, that man has a major problem. In his mind (or actually, on top of his mind) is something he thinks will forever keep him from finishing first in life, or even from coming in a strong second. It's something that is the reason, he believes, every relationship has been ruined.

For whatever reason, he couldn't picture a successful future for himself without thick, curly locks of hair. And by picking out something in his life that he was powerless to change and seeing it as the source of all his problems, he was directly limiting his entire future.

While that example may seem dramatic, there are so many people who have chosen a life based on learned helplessness. They're convinced that they missed something in the past, and that lack has the power to block any growth in their future.

Where does such thinking come from? Usually, some trauma in the past has convinced us to become a pessimist, believing that "fate" has already dealt us a losing hand and we're powerless to make changes that will really count.

Remember our helpless and hopeless friend in the very first chapter who, along with so many others today, was looking at life as hopeless and the future as "settled science" against us. But even when we're facing challenges, God absolutely has a "future and a hope" (Jeremiah 29:11) for us.

> **Even when we're facing challenges, God absolutely has a "future and a hope" for us.**

How common is this problem? As I said earlier, such fatalism is epidemic, particularly among those who are so young and have their whole life in front of them!

Again, the problem isn't usually something like our hair. For most men at least, the difference between a good haircut and a bad one is about a week. And the rest of us are thankful for whatever hair we have left and whatever color it's becoming!

But take a long look in the mirror and ask yourself if you've defined your future according to any of the following:

- If I had married _____, things would have been different.
- If I had chosen college instead of my trade, I wouldn't be in the situation I'm in now.
- If my parents had stayed together . . .
- If my pastor hadn't fallen . . .
- If my coach had just played me . . .
- If my company hadn't transferred me . . .
- If my car hadn't been in that accident . . .
- If my father had just given me the help he gave my brother . . .

One thing that causes us to be helpless is thinking that if just . . . if just . . . if just . . . whatever hadn't happened, then we could change. But because it did, we're helpless to do anything.

Are there any decisions you've made in life that make you feel the key to change is only in the past? Then put that card or post up on your LifeMap. And ask yourself if there are other ways we can choose helplessness over hopefulness.

We can choose helplessness when we feel there's no way of escape.

Back in the 1970s at the University of Pennsylvania, Dr. Martin Seligman did studies on what caused people (and animals) to feel helpless. He learned that helplessness was a practiced way of viewing the future that keeps you dependent on the past.[3]

Experiencing a major trauma—from losing a spouse to losing a job to losing your parents' blessing—affects a person deeply. For some of us, such an event not only marks our past, but it also can immobilize us as we face the future.

Instead of actively believing we have the inner resources and determination to solve our problems, we can become passive, dependent, and depressed with the first barrier that goes up. In short, we learn that in the face of pain, where escape seems hopeless, we should just give up.

Think about this in terms of people you've seen who have tried and failed or who feel as if no matter what happens, they can't change.

Ask yourself (or the person you're helping create their LifeMap) if there was a time when some significant emotional event caused you to think you could never escape the pain or move forward. If so, that should go on a card under Emotional Freeze Points or Individual Flash Points.

We can choose helplessness if we feel our effort doesn't match our achievement.

If you practice learned helplessness, there is the feeling that no matter what you do, your effort won't match your achievement. Unfortunately, in our fallen world, sometimes that statement rings true. Take Todd, for example.

For five years, he worked his way up from bagging groceries to ordering them as assistant manager. He put in countless weekends and unquestioned overtime, and he always gave an accurate accounting at closing time. If anyone deserved the promotion to store manager at the new megastore, it was Todd. And that's just what he was verbally promised.

Todd's diligent work stood out, but he never counted on

what happened. The absentee owner decided his nephew was cut out for leadership. And with no notice to Todd's superiors, and no experience on the nephew's part, that unqualified man was given the position.

What about Todd? He was given the grand opportunity to move to the new store and train the person who would be sitting in the glass office where he should have sat.

That was nine years ago, and Todd has never been the same since. After two bitter years of enduring emotional pain every day, he left the grocery business for an unsuccessful run at college. After failing at that—and finally his marriage—his life slowed down to a crawl. He's in construction now, but every rent payment is a struggle, and every suggestion to open a door of change is slammed shut.

Why try? is Todd's attitude. After all, it's the breaks that make you, not backbreaking work. He already tried that and got nothing but disappointment. He learned the hard way that effort doesn't equal achievement.

It's true that effort sometimes doesn't bring the rewards we desire. So here's where we ask someone in the LifeMapping process if there's anything in their past (a key emotional event) where they felt as though no matter how hard they tried, it didn't matter. Nothing would change.

It is amazing how you'll see people's eyes open as they think back to times when the pain of their efforts not being rewarded impacted their lives.

We can choose helplessness if we feel someone has stolen the only key to genuine change.

Brian was the older of two brothers. If his father should have bonded with anyone, he figured, it should have been him, not his younger brother. He wore his heart out to please his father. But no matter how far he stretched toward him, he could never reach the arms of acceptance he wanted so much. Instead, he grew up watching his younger brother and father bond ever closer together.

In a climate of unfair comparison and favoritism, Brian made a subtle but terribly damaging decision. Deep inside, he equated what he was missing with what he could never become—younger. And because he focused on something that could never happen as his sole key to future happiness, he became a committed pessimist . . . and eventually sank into clinical depression. Here's why trying to surface and—if it's there—deal with this post on a LifeMap is so important: In studies of pessimists, they persistently look *backward*.[4]

For example, pessimists consistently grow up wanting to be younger, like Brian; optimists grow up looking forward and wishing they were older. By never being able to "forget what lies behind" (Philippians 3:13), pessimists stay stuck in their pain rather than pushing forward to a positive future.

If you feel your effort doesn't match your achievement, that the only key to happiness is forever out of reach, or that someone else has the *only* thing that makes life livable, those all need to go on your LifeMap.

I'm All Alone in My Pain

People who are trapped in learned helplessness carry something else as well—the belief that no one is coming to help, that no one will reach back when they reach out. And after enough time of believing this, they can even become oblivious to outside encouragement when it finally comes.

Take Pam, who grew up on the mission field. When it came to discipline, her father wasn't just strict—he was severe. One Sunday when she was nine years old, for example, she was sitting next to a friend at the back of the church, whispering about something they were going to do after the service.

In the middle of his sermon, her father called out Pam's name and ordered her to come up front. Before the entire congregation, he laid into her about how disrespectful and dishonoring she was being in church. Then he took her outside (in full view of the congregation through the windows) and gave her an embarrassing and humiliating whipping that she has never forgotten.

Many years later, when Pam's marriage began crumbling, her pain called forth echoes from the past. Wrapped in the powerlessness she had felt as a child, she grew almost comatose when it came to listening to her husband's complaints or receiving any counsel.

Many people who have gone through trauma beat a hasty inner retreat when they see painful situations coming. Instead of being open to counsel or hearing others' offers of help, they pull further and further inside, isolating themselves more and more and cutting themselves off from genuine help. Not because it isn't being offered but because they don't believe it is real!

Such a deep sense of impenetrable loneliness can lead to disaster. Among those who share that mindset are many compulsive gamblers, sexaholics, alcoholics, and abusive parents or spouses. Convinced deep inside that there is no escape from their pain, they abuse a drug or practice a pattern of behavior that's familiar (their being abused) or that will somehow deaden the pain. But they only compound their pain in the process and get further mired in their problems.

The book of Proverbs has much to say about the "lazy" and the "fool," both models for learned helplessness. One of the verses that applies shows the foolishness of inner isolation: "One who separates himself [from God and others] seeks his own desire; he quarrels against all sound wisdom" (Proverbs 18:1). And the final result of having no future: "The lazy one buries his hand in the dish, but will not even bring it back to his mouth" (Proverbs 19:24).

Have you given over your future to some unpredictable fate, not to consistent effort? Does some missing key keep the door locked to change in your life? Are you hard of hearing when it comes to accepting or even asking for sound counsel?

If you answer yes, you're right where the enemy wants you. Instead of following a LifeMap headed toward fullness of life in Christ, you're following a dead-end trail toward fractured relationships and an unfulfilled life.

But there is hope! It may take time with a godly counselor or Christian life coach, but you can move past helplessness. You can, as we learned at the start of the chapter, practice learned hopefulness and see it help you overcome those barriers that currently hold you back from real change. As we'll see in the next chapter, you can also use memorial markers to reinforce your past successes, new commitments, and positive outlook on life.

Digging Deeper

1. Describe a time in your life when you worked hard to achieve something only to have your efforts go unrewarded as a result of events beyond your control. What was your reaction?

2. When thinking about your life, do you tend to focus on the past or the future?

3. Jeremiah 29:11 is a familiar passage that talks about God's perspective regarding our future. Review this verse and use it as a springboard in asking God to shape your attitude about your future.

CHAPTER 12

Memorial Markers

As OUR LOOK at LifeMapping nears an end, it's my hope that you are more aware of where you've come from, more certain about where you're going, and more confident that the Lord Jesus has been with you through every freeze point, every flash point, and every twist and transition in your life. It's my hope, too, that you've mapped out a positive plan for your future, with a prayed-over purpose surrounded by commitment and conviction and the willingness to choose learned hopefulness and work to anticipate challenges.

But there's one final element of LifeMapping that needs to be explored. If learned hopefulness can help you deal with problems that might throw you off course, *memorial markers* can add incredibly powerful everyday objects or pictures that provide hope that your future is indeed in God's hands—and it's a positive future.

But what exactly do I mean by a memorial marker? It's a concept as old as the Exodus.

Joshua's First Day on the Job

Do you have a good first-day-on-the-job story? Joshua certainly did. The Lord woke him with the challenge to lead the entire nation of Israel across the Jordan River at flood stage—without getting wet. The assignment wasn't for Joshua to build a bridge but to trust in the same God who had once before parted the waters for Israel to pass through.

Actually, Joshua was getting a second chance to follow a LifeMap that had been handed to Moses and the rest of his generation. If you'll recall, Moses called on Pharaoh to "let My people go" (see Exodus 5:1). Finally, after a series of plagues, they did escape from Egypt. But as they came to the Red Sea, Pharaoh's heart hardened again, and he raced after the fleeing Israelites to kill them. That was not to be, and in one of the greatest miracles recorded in the Scriptures, almighty God parted the sea to let His people go free, and then He crashed the water down on top of the pursuing Egyptians.

Can you imagine the incredible sight those people saw that day? God's power miraculously intervened to save them. And later, they would see God's power sustain them with water to drink and manna to eat.

But even a steady dose of miracles didn't increase the people's faith. Remember their response to the report of the twelve spies who had gone ahead to scope out the

Promised Land? Ten of the spies (I dare you to remember any of their names) brought back a bad report of giants in the land and an unconquerable enemy dead ahead. Only two of the twelve—Joshua and Caleb (lots of people name their sons after them)—remembered a God who could destroy an army of Egyptians, complete with iron chariots, and who would fight for them now.

But the pessimism of the ten spies would prevail. And in God's judgment on their lack of faith, all the people of that generation except Joshua and Caleb would die without entering the Promised Land.

Now it was time for a second chance at God's first choice.

Joshua had already been in the Promised Land once, and he didn't hesitate to go back. This time, however, there were a few more lunches to pack than twelve. The Ark of the Covenant went ahead of him, and then the entire nation followed. As the robes of the priests dipped in the Jordan, the waters of the flooded river stopped up in a heap upstream—an incredible miracle no less marvelous than that first parting years before.

That's the story of what happened when Joshua entered the land. Let me make two applications, and then we'll look at what happened next that involves memorial markers.

Don't Be Too Hard on Those Early Israelites

It's easy to judge those "faithless" Israelites who froze up instead of following God into the Promised Land. But we know from experience and research that a painful, inescapable situation typically produces a condition of helplessness in a person.

Where had the nation of Israel just come from? Slavery—painful, inescapable, brutal slavery. Little or no straw to make their bricks. A life where they learned that nothing they could do would free them and nothing they could say ever counted. That's a climate where a feeling of helplessness would develop easily.

That all changed, however, when Moses revealed the power and love of a mighty God. The people now had every reason to hope. But when the trials came, where did they want to head? Forward toward God and learned hopefulness? No, they wanted to go backward toward Egypt and again take their fill of leeks and garlic. In fact, several times they begged Moses to let them go back to slavery instead of moving forward to the Promised Land.

Without a doubt, people can be swayed from their hope. Just ask the people of Israel who never got to go into the Promised Land. Or ask Peter, who denied Jesus three times after swearing he would die first.

But people can come back. Peter, indeed, turned into that rock Jesus had pictured him to be, and the next generation of Israelites didn't complain—they got up and moved out when Joshua said, "Let's go!"

One Major Difference between the Two Partings

Many similarities exist between the parting of the Red Sea and the parting of the Jordan. Both confirmed a man, in the eyes of all the people, in the leadership role God had given him. Both were mighty demonstrations that God's power was with Moses and Joshua from the first day of their ministries. But there was one difference.

"This shall be a sign among you; when your children ask later, saying, 'What do these stones mean to you?' then you shall say to them, 'That the waters of the Jordan were cut off before the ark of the covenant of the LORD; when it crossed the Jordan, the waters of the Jordan were cut off.' So these stones shall become a memorial to the sons of Israel forever."

JOSHUA 4:6-7

Namely, after Joshua had gone through the waters, God had him go back. Actually, God had him send twelve men back to the Jordan, and this time they were to pick up twelve stones (one for each Hebrew tribe) from the middle of the dry riverbed as a testimony of God's power and purpose.

Those stones would become a memorial marker—a clear picture that would remind young and old that yes, indeed, God had worked in a mighty way that day and was working in their lives still.

That's a great story, but what does it have to do with LifeMapping?

Plenty!

So far, you've pinned up cards that represent strengths, successes, and "high hill" people. You've pictured freeze points, flash points, and untied transitions. You've dealt with image management issues, forged goals for the major areas of your life, and even been challenged to keep commitment, self-control, and your clear plan ahead of you by practicing learned hopefulness.

> Those stones would become a memorial marker—a clear picture that would remind young and old that yes, indeed, God had worked in a mighty way that day and was working in their lives still.

But one thing is missing. It's a tangible reminder of the process you've been through. It's a memorial marker that can give you a picture of all you can become. It's something that has proven to be a great help to Jim and Susan.

The Real Thing

Jim had taken image management to new heights, primarily by not telling his wife, Susan, that he'd been married before. Their trust level instantly went from rock solid to rubble when she learned the truth. Restoring their relationship took time, lots of counseling, and finally, Susan's willingness to forgive. But they got through the storm together. A LifeMap and this eighth element of the tool cemented their changed hearts, minds, and goals.

When the time came for their last counseling appointment, I had something wrapped up to give them. I passed it across the table, and they opened it with questioning looks. Once the package was open, they had even more questions.

Inside the package was a nice oak frame with nonglare glass covering two matted dollar bills. At least they *looked* like dollar bills. But upon closer examination, Jim and Susan saw that the top bill was actually a counterfeit (one I'd ripped off from my kids' playroom), while the bottom bill was the real thing. And the reason for the difference wasn't just that I'm cheap.

Do you see how those two bills might be a memorial marker for them?

What was the main problem they had when they first came in? Jim was being a phony. That's why the top dollar bill was a counterfeit. It looked good from a distance, but you couldn't cash it in, even on a toy. That bill was a picture of what Jim had been.

The crisp, fresh-from-the-mint bill on the bottom was the real thing, however. The "real thing" was what Jim wanted so much to be and what Susan struggled so hard to believe he could become.

Those dollar bills were like twelve stones from a river. They pictured where they had been, what God had done for them, and what He promised to do in their future. That picture still hangs in their home today. And they made another one that hangs in his office. Everyone thinks it's the first two dollars he made with his company. It's actually a picture, at work and at home, that he needs to stay committed to authentic living rather than image management—a commitment he's honored now for decades.

All kinds of objects, pictures, or even animals or plants might serve as your memorial markers. (For a list of more possibilities, turn to the appendix.) But here's the story of one special memorial marker I've carried with me.

When a Letter Becomes a Memorial Marker

If you run into me at a conference or at the airport and I've got my backpack with me, feel free to ask to see *that letter*. It's not a letter from Cindy, even though I carry her picture with me everywhere. It's a letter from Great-Uncle Max.

We didn't meet until I was in college, but he's my father's uncle. My great-uncle. Over the years, we built a steady, growing relationship. He was the one who told me about my father's past, which helped me both understand and forgive Dad. And I sat with Uncle Max at the hospital for two days straight when his wife was run over by a wrecker and lived to tell about it.

Between those times of trial, Uncle Max loved me, grudgingly adopted me, and most of all let me adopt him. He looked so much like my father (all the Trents have that look), but I could laugh with him, cry with him, and even give him a hug—things I could never do with my own father.

As his health was failing, Uncle Max sent me a letter, asking if I would be the executor of his living will. That meant that I would be the one to say, "No medical heroics." While it was a sad acknowledgment of his advancing years (eighty-six at the time of writing), it contains one line that has caused me to carry it every day since.

For a young boy who always wanted a father—who grew up with a LifeMap that had a missing place where that significant person should have been—what Uncle Max said in that letter brought tears to my eyes and a sense of closure to my heart. Here's what he wrote with a shaky hand on paper that's now well creased:

> Thank you, John. You have helped me so much in
> the past, and I am sure you will continue to do so.
> Because you are my son.
> Affectionately, Max.

I had grown up with a hole in my heart. My own father never gave me his blessing or called me his son. But now I had Uncle Max's word on it. I was *his* son.

I don't know what memorial markers you'll come up with

as you look over your LifeMap. Again, you'll find lots of examples in the appendix of those that other people have come up with.

Perhaps you'll pick a sturdy mantel clock that pictures a stable past and a precision-crafted future. It might be a ceramic rose that forever blooms now that you know Jesus, the rose of Sharon. It might be that bookmark your son made at camp that says, *World's Best Mom. I love you, Jimmy.*

Whatever your memorial markers turn out to be, it's amazing how powerful they can be as tangible pictures of your desire to map out a positive, God-honoring future.

That brings us to the end of your journey through this book to create your LifeMap. But please turn the page as Kari (our older daughter) and I share with you one last challenge and blessing.

Digging Deeper

1. As a reminder of what you've just read, what is the purpose of a memorial marker? How can it help you in the LifeMapping process?

2. From your own reading of the Bible, can you list two other occasions when God gave His people memorial markers? (You might look in the book of Genesis at the stories of Abraham and Noah.)

3. What key events or goals in your life would you like to always remember? What would be appropriate memorial markers for those events? (See the appendix for some great ideas.)

4. In his book *Choosing to Live the Blessing*, Dr. Trent points out that people remember "pictures" (important moments and memories). Can you think of a tangible memorial marker that could be a picture of your love for someone close to you (e.g., a plaque he or she could hang on the wall, a poem you wrote for him or her, or a memento from a trip or vacation that evokes positive memories)?

CHAPTER 13

A Challenge to Be a LifeMapping® Coach to Others

CONGRATULATIONS FOR GOING through all the work in creating your LifeMap! You've surfaced your strengths and celebrated those "high hill" people who have meant so much. You've looked hard at your freeze points and flash points, even the untied transitions that were there as well. You've taken the first steps in laying out a positive plan toward a special future. And you're protected by that choice to keep moving forward by embracing learned hopefulness. Finally, you've captured in a memorial marker something that no one else might understand, but it's a physical picture or object that gives you a tangible reminder of God's presence in your life. *All* your life.

If you've come this far, we know you've expended so much energy, effort, insight, prayers, and perhaps even tears in crafting your LifeMap. We pray, as you've worked through each element of LifeMapping, that you've gotten a better picture of your life story. And that you've also had your eyes opened to see the One who has walked beside you every step of your journey.

God gave you all those strengths and gifts you've lived out. And we want to end this book by reminding you that you were given those strengths in part so you can help others. Thus, our call now is for you to consider doing something great.

A Challenge to Do Something Great

If there was ever a time when people needed help and hope, it's today. The thing that is most under attack in our day is any view that God has a special, positive future for us.

So we want to set a challeng before you: Don't just finish your LifeMap, but also prayerfully consider helping someone else with what you've learned and experienced. Whether it's your spouse, your adult child, a close friend, or a small group of special someones, we challenge you to guide him or her through this experience you've been through. Someone who needs help in seeing his or her strengths. Or in dealing with past hurts. Or in making a decision for truth and authentic living. Or who needs to get a clear plan in the most important areas of his or her life. Or who needs to choose to be resilient and hopeful as he or she deals with the things that could blow up that plan. And who would even benefit from a memorial marker, as you have, to cement God's presence in the midst of it all.

That's the challenge. Go back through this with someone you love and care about. Don't just put the book on the shelf now that you're done. Rather, use it to encourage someone else who needs a different, hopeful, God- and life-honoring picture of a hopeful future when so many see none.

You might even want to consider getting training as a life coach. A huge part of what we do at StrongFamilies.com is to help train such coaches. We do that through what we think is the most helpful Christian coaching portal on the planet.

> **Don't just finish your LifeMap, but also prayerfully consider helping someone else with what you've learned and experienced.**

What's a life coach?

It's someone who isn't a state-licensed counselor but gets some deeper training in what our friend Dr. Tony Wheeler calls "coffee cup coaching." It means developing skills in walking well with others through life and in sharing this message of LifeMapping. If that sounds like something God may be tapping you on the shoulder to do, then start by going to the website of ICCI, the International Christian Coaching Institute (ICCIcoaching.com).

At that site, you'll find information on how you can become a StrongFamilies coach. You do that by taking three courses. In them, we teach people like you to help others get a clear picture of their past and build a prayed-over, positive plan for the future ("Becoming a LifeMapping Coach"). We train coaches to help others fill in those "What are my strengths?" blanks on their LifeMaps ("Becoming a Strengths Coach"). And we equip coaches to help men and women build and maintain a secure base of connection and attachment with the Lord and with their loved ones ("Becoming a Blessing and Attachment Coach").

We'd love to have you be a champion in helping people

see their strengths, gain a clear plan toward God's best, and receive a blessing, perhaps for the first time in their lives.

And now, as we close, let us give *you* a blessing.

A Blessing for You

In Old Testament times, you never let someone you loved go farther than the horizon (roughly eleven miles) without putting a blessing on them. Words of God's love, of high value and a special future, were spoken over someone whom you hoped to see again. But no matter what the future held, they would have those words of blessing on them—words helping them know they had great value and weren't alone in their journey.

That's what we'd like to do for you right now.

It's likely you're reading this book more than eleven miles from Scottsdale, Arizona, where I (John) live, or Seattle, Washington, where Kari lives. But even if we're neighbors, we'd like to put this blessing on you right now.

Imagine that we're standing in front of you with a hand on your shoulder. (If you come to one of our ICCI conferences, this is just what we do.) Now we pray this blessing over you:

Lord Jesus, thank You so much for this person who has read all the way through this book. Even more, who has stepped into the challenge of laying out his or her story by building out a LifeMap. Lord, may this person have seen You in every one of those eight elements of LifeMapping—from the strengths You've given to the struggles the person has had. Those wonderful "high hill" people you placed in his or her life. And those people who may have needed to be forgiven or their words put aside, replaced by words of love and life that You, Lord, speak over them.

And now, Lord, this person has a plan that's been prayed over. We ask You to bless every bit of it and give the wisdom and courage to anticipate the challenges and keep pressing forward toward that high calling You give us of loving You and leading others to You.

Lord, help this person to know none of us were called to do life alone. That there are people who need him or her to speak truth and blessing and wisdom from Your Word into their lives. For all this person experiences in the days ahead, may You give this person great favor to find a clear path toward a special future and toward You.

These are crazy, chaotic times, Lord, full of personal turmoil. May this person always remember that in Your presence is fullness of joy, and that in that place of closeness to You, we can indeed live and move into a place of purposeful calm because of all You've done for us.

We pray all this in Your name, Jesus.

Amen.

John Trent
Kari Trent Stageberg
StrongFamilies.com

Your LifeMap® Template

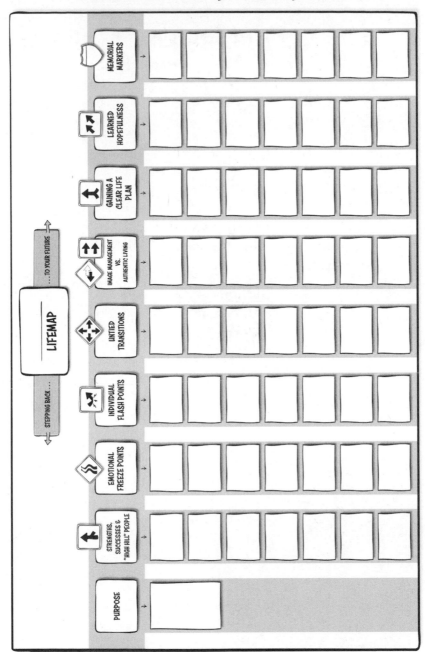

Print Charts

Use the QR code to view and
print charts from this book in PDF form.

Appendix

23 Memorial Markers Others Have Used

OVER THE YEARS, as I've worked with couples and singles, I've kept a list of their everyday memorial markers. If the concept of memorial markers is new to you, take time to read through the following descriptions for ideas that can easily be within your reach. These real-life suggestions may help you think of something that makes your commitment, goal, or desire for change more concrete.

1. "Our memorial marker is a ceramic inkwell with a long quill pen. We bought this together and leave it sitting out on the desk in our bedroom. Each day when we see it, it reminds us that, by God's grace, we're able to write a new page in our life story."

2. "For my marker, I splurged and bought a real nice, wooden duck decoy. What it represents to me is a rough piece of wood that a skilled hand lovingly carved and painted until it looks as if it could come alive. That's what the Lord has done for me . . . cutting away the rough edges and bringing me to life. I leave

it sitting out at work, and it's a great reminder of who He's helping me to become."

3. My good friend Tim Kimmel has a wonderful memorial marker I explain with his permission. On top of his rolltop desk, he has two small pictures that sit on opposite sides of a large picture of his wife and children. The picture on the left is a photo of the hospital where Tim was born. The one on the right is a photo of the Kimmel family cemetery plot, where Tim will one day be laid to rest. In between where he came from and where he'll end up is that photo of Darcy, his wife, and their four kids. This display graphically reminds him of where he started, where he's heading, and what's important while he's alive.

4. "It's a small thing, but our memorial marker is a wooden clothespin with the words *God's love* handwritten on it. It's a reminder that no matter how hectic things get, His love is what holds everything together for us."

5. "My husband and I brought back a fairly large piece of coral from our once-in-a-lifetime trip to Hawaii. The marker reminds us of our commitment to take 'five-minute vacations' from our hectic schedules."

6. "Jayne and I have an unusual memorial marker that means the world to us. Two years ago, I was between jobs, and our savings had been totally depleted. We were facing the certain loss of our home. That's when an unmarked envelope came with two months' house payment inside. That made the difference between us

keeping or losing our house. We feel certain it was someone from our church, but we still don't know for sure today. We framed that envelope as a reminder of how faithful God has been to us."

7. "My memorial marker is a small, antique, red wagon that I've turned into a coffee table in my home. It's not pretty anymore, but it's sturdy and reliable and gaining more value as an antique every day. And by the way, I'm a senior citizen. That wagon reminds me of my continued worth to God and others as I get older."

8. "The marker I use is something I know meant the world to my grandfather. It's his old, folding carpenter's ruler, all scratched and weather-beaten. I keep it on top of my desk as a reminder of the godly heritage he left me. He always walked the straight and narrow, and it's a reminder to me to be a man of integrity."

9. "I decided to carry a pocket watch instead of a wristwatch to remind me of my commitment to my God and family. I had engraved on the outside my wife's and son's initials, plus my favorite passage, Joshua 1:8-9. It's a hassle sometimes to have to reach into my pocket to look for the time, but it always reminds me of what's most important to me when I do."

10. "Our memorial marker has to do with adding more 'softness' to the way we treat each other. We each bought one of those extra-soft teddy bears as softness reminders. Not only have they worked, but having stuffed animals on my bed also makes me feel like a kid again!"

11. "I have a fishing lure hanging in my sewing room, framed in a shadow box. While I don't fish, it's a reminder of all the times my father spent with me when I was young, fishing. It makes me think of the time he gave up for me and of how I want to be there for my children."

12. "We went through the terrible experience of a two-year-long lawsuit. There were days when we not only wanted to give up, but we questioned God as well. We found our memorial marker at the mall after a really tough day. We were walking through a shop when my husband and I both saw a ceramic bulldog dressed up to look like Winston Churchill. When we both stopped laughing, we bought it, and it was a great reminder to us to have the tenacity of a bulldog to get through that lawsuit—and we did!"

13. "While nobody else would pick out my memorial marker, I see it every time I pull open the bathroom medicine chest. There, amidst my shaver and various sprays, is a bottle of Old Spice aftershave. It's empty except for its lingering smell. But it was my father's last bottle of aftershave, and it makes me think of him. I keep it to remind me that I'm building memories for my kids every day."

14. "After learning about LifeMapping and memorial markers, I thought of something I needed to change, and I ran into a picture of my commitment at the mall. I was going by a knife shop and saw a beautiful pocketknife with a carved handle. Now I carry a

constant reminder to 'cut out' one particular negative pattern from the past."

15. "My marker is a miniature brass telescope. It reminds me to focus attention on important issues like my relationship with Christ and my family. You'd be surprised how many people ask about it as it lies on my desk, and I get to cement my commitment all over again in telling them!"

16. "My grandmother's wire-rimmed glasses are what I use to remind me of my commitment to be more like Christ. She had blue, piercing eyes that her glasses didn't dim a bit, and she was a model of someone committed to God's service. Just having them on my dresser at home is a reminder to be like her and to be all I can become for the Lord."

17. "While it's nothing spectacular, our memorial marker is a large seashell we picked up on a trip to Hawaii several years ago. It's one of those fluted shells, where you can put it up to your ear and still 'hear' the ocean's roar. This reminds us that our children will remember—and be able to play back—the words we say to them. Years from now, we want the sound others hear coming from their lives to be a pleasing sound and memory."

18. "It's shut down now, but I used to live near an iron smelter. My marker is a 5 × 7 picture that sits on my desk of that old plant running at full steam, with the sparks and red glow of molten iron being poured out. It's my desire that God purify and melt away the

impurities in my life as well, so that I can be someone who supports others and stands the test of time."

19. "At our wedding, a wealthy friend of my father's gave us a genuine Waterford crystal paperweight. For a long time, we just put it away because our house was mostly antiques. But after learning about memorial markers, we took it out to remind us to treat each other and the children as *extremely valuable . . .* and *very fragile.*"

20. "After your conference where you talked about LifeMapping, my husband came up with our memorial marker. He's in land development and often commissions an aerial photograph to be taken of a tract of land he's considering purchasing. We talked about it, and he had a pilot go up and take an aerial view of our neighborhood! That's our reminder that we need to think and pray not just for our house but for our neighbors and community around us as well."

21. "I was driving past my old neighborhood several months ago when I saw my memorial marker. Due to redistricting, the area getting older, and fewer people having kids in that section of town, they tore down my old grade school. I stopped the car while they were demolishing it, went over, and picked up a brick. To everyone else it's just an old brick, but to me, it's a reminder that I'm from the 'old school,' where commitment, honor, and love meant something. It's also a reminder that if I let anger or dishonor enter my home, it can tear my home down the way my school was torn down."

22. "I come from a family where favoritism was practiced. I know what it's like to feel left out, and that's why I chose a small brass measuring scale like the legal scales you see. I bought two small weights that weigh the same and put them on each side of the scale so they're balanced there. That's a picture to me of my goal in blessing my children—to keep things in balance as much as I can so my kids don't feel the way I did."

23. "My memorial marker is a small piece of rusted iron I picked up. I've struggled with anger a lot, and I'm finally committed to getting the help and support I need to control it. That rusted iron is a reminder that anger can rust what's precious to me (like my marriage) if I don't get help."

Notes

CHAPTER 1: FROM PERSONAL CHAOS TO PURPOSEFUL CALM

1. Alison Abbot, "COVID's Mental Health Toll: How Scientists Are Tracking a Surge in Depression," *Nature*, February 3, 2021, https://www.nature.com/articles/d41586-021-00175-z.
2. Caroline Hickman et al., "Climate Anxiety in Children and Young People and Their Beliefs about Government Responses to Climate Change: A Global Survey," *The Lancet Planetary Health* 5, no. 12 (December 1, 2021), e863–e873, https://pubmed.ncbi.nlm.nih.gov/34895496.
3. "ICCI Credentialing," International Christian Coaching Institute (website), https://iccicoaching.com/credentialing.

CHAPTER 2: WHAT IS LIFEMAPPING*?

1. *A Christmas Carol* by Charles Dickens was first published in 1843.
2. Viktor E. Frankl, *Man's Search for Meaning* (New York: Simon & Schuster, 1984), 81, 83.

CHAPTER 3: HOW LIFEMAPPING* BEGAN

1. Deborah E. Gorton, *Embracing Uncomfortable: Facing Our Fears While Pursuing Our Purpose* (Chicago: Northfield Publishing, 2020).¶
2. Many good books describe Leonardo da Vinci's art and graphic design approach. See, for example, Jack Wasserman, *Leonardo da Vinci* (New York: Harry N. Abrams, 1984), 8.
3. Bob Thomas, *Disney's Art of Animation: From Mickey Mouse to Beauty and the Beast* (New York: Hyperion/Welcome Enterprises, 1991), 15.

CHAPTER 5: RECOGNIZING YOUR STRENGTHS, SUCCESSES, AND "HIGH HILL" PEOPLE

1. Robert Karasek and Töres Theorell, *Healthy Work* (New York: Basic Books, 1990), 12–21.

2. Debbie, "Weighing In on Legalism," *Two Minutes of Grace* (blog), December 1, 2012, https://www.twominutesofgrace.wordpress.com/2012/12/01/weighing-in-on-legalism.

3. *Chariots of Fire*, directed by Hugh Hudson (Burbank, CA: Warner Bros., 1981).

4. Donald O. Clifton and Paula Nelson, *Soar with Your Strengths* (New York: Delacourte, 1992), 23.

5. Don Rheem, *Thrive by Design: The Neuroscience That Drives High-Performance Cultures* (Charleston, SC: Forbes Books, 2017), 36–37, Kindle.

6. Adapted from Jack Canfield and Mark Victor Hansen, *Chicken Soup for the Soul* (Boca Raton, FL: Health Communications, 1993), 125–28.

CHAPTER 6: EMOTIONAL FREEZE POINTS

1. Latrobe Carroll, "Willa Sibert Cather," The *Willa Cather Archive*, https://cather.unl.edu/writings/bohlke/interviews/bohlke.i.15.

2. Christopher Peterson and Lisa M. Bossio, *Health and Optimism* (Glencoe, IL: The Free Press, 1991), 2; see table 1-1, "Historical Perspective on Optimism Versus Pessimism."

3. C. Peterson, M. Seligman, and G. Vaillant, "Pessimistic Explanatory Style Is a Risk Factor for Physical Illness," *Journal of Personality and Social Psychology* 55, no. 1 (July 1988), 23–27, https://pubmed.ncbi.nlm.nih.gov/3418489.

4. C. Peterson, D. Colvin, and E. Lin, "Explanatory Style and Helplessness," unpublished manuscript, University of Michigan, reported in Peterson and Bossio, *Health and Optimism*, 34.

5. "Optimism Associated with Lower Risk of Heart Failure," University of Michigan News, April 8, 2014. Accessed May 3, 2023, https://news.umich.edu/optimism-associated-with-lower-risk-of-heart-failure.

6. Hans J. Eysenck, "Personality and Stress as Causal Factors in Cancer and Coronary Heart Disease," in M. P. Janisse, ed., *Individual Differences, Stress, and Health Psychology* (New York: Springer-Verlag, 1988), 121–27.

7. Robert S. Desowitz, *The Thorn in the Starfish* (New York: Norton, 1987), 91.

8. John Gottman, *Why Marriages Succeed or Fail* (New York: Simon & Schuster, 1994), 20.

9. Dicke, Amy Kristine, "Optimism and Its Effect on Romantic Relationships," Dissertation in Psychology, Texas Tech University, 1997, Texas Digital Library 2014, https://ttu-ir.tdl.org/bitstream/handle/2346/13346/31295012488952.pdf?sequence=1. See also Conversano, Ciro, et al, "Optimism and Its Impact on Mental and Physical Well-Being," NIH Study, https://www.ncbi.nlm.nih.gov/pmc/articles/PMC2894461.

10. For a good description of "pessimism bias," read the Decision Lab article titled, "Why do we think we're destined to fail?" https://thedecisionlab.com /biases/pessimism-bias.

11. Jane B. Burka and Lenora M. Yuen, *Procrastination: Why You Do It, What to Do about It Now* (Boston: Da Capo Lifelong Books, 2008), 13–17, 270.

CHAPTER 7: INDIVIDUAL FLASH POINTS

1. C. Robert Jennings, "Dr. Seuss: 'What am I doing here?'" Saturday Evening Post, February 10, 2016, http://www.saturdayeveningpost.com/2016/02 /dr-seuss.

CHAPTER 8: UNTIED TRANSITIONS

1. For a more complete account of that experience with my father and the lesson God taught me in the process, see Gary Smalley and John Trent, *The Gift of the Blessing* (Nashville: Thomas Nelson, 1993), especially chapter 11, "When You Know You Will Never Receive a Parent's Blessing."

2. Simon Moore, "How Long Will Your Retirement Really Last?" *Forbes*, April 24, 2018, https://www.forbes.com/sites/simonmoore/2018/04/24 /how-long-will-your-retirement-last/?sh=175bb7117472.

CHAPTER 10: GAINING A CLEAR LIFE PLAN

1. All the books in this series are published by Thomas Nelson.

2. Matt Bradshaw and Blake Victor Kent, "Prayer, Attachment to God, and Changes in Psychological Well-Being in Later Life," *Journal of Aging and Health* 30, no. 5 (2018), https://www.journals.sagepub.com/doi /full/10.1177/0898264316688116.

CHAPTER 11: LEARNED HELPLESSNESS VS. LEARNED HOPEFULNESS

1. For the Draveckys' inspiring story, see their book Dave and Jan Dravecky (with Ken Gire), *When You Can't Come Back* (New York: HarperCollins, 1992); or see Dave Dravecky (with Tim Stafford), *Comeback* (Grand Rapids, MI: Zondervan, 1992).

2. "Not Letting the Birds Nest in Our Hair," *Lutheran Press*, October 18, 2016, https://lutheranpress.com/2016/10/18/not-letting-the-birds-nest -in-our-hair.

3. Christopher Peterson and Lisa M. Bossio, *Health and Optimism* (Glencoe, IL: The Free Press, 1991), 91; and Martin E. P. Seligman, *Learned Optimism: How to Change Your Mind and Life* (New York: Vintage Books, 2006), 69.

4. Peterson and Bossio, *Health and Optimism*, 77. See also Hugo, "Here's Why You're a Pessimist (7 Ways to Stop Being Pessimistic)," January 29, 2023, https://www.trackinghappiness.com/how-to-stop-being-pessimistic.

Ready to Take That Next Step and Become a Certified "Where Do I Go from Here?" LifeMapping® Coach?

If you've found help and encouragement from creating your own LifeMap—consider taking that next step in helping others do the same!

If you're already a Life Coach or "people helper" or if you want to become one, Dr. Trent and Kari Trent Stageberg have joined with ICCI (International Christian Coaching Institute) to create three courses for Life Coaches and "people helpers." One course is on becoming a Blessing and Attachment Coach. Another is on becoming a StrongFamilies Strength Coach (using Dr. Trent's animal personality model from *The Two Sides of Love*). And the third is a course on becoming a certified "Where Do I Go from Here?" LifeMapping® Coach!

For more information, go to iccicoaching.com/product /relationship-and-attachment-coaching-lifemapping.

You can also go to StrongFamilies.com and click on the "Coaching" button.

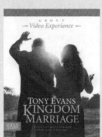
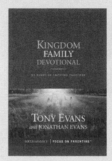

THE KINGDOM SERIES
FROM DR. TONY EVANS

MORE RESOURCES TO GROW YOUR FAITH AND FURTHER GOD'S KINGDOM!

KINGDOM MAN
978-1-58997-685-6

KINGDOM MAN
DEVOTIONAL
978-1-62405-121-0

KINGDOM WOMAN
978-1-58997-743-3

KINGDOM WOMAN
DEVOTIONAL
978-1-62405-122-7

KINGDOM WOMAN
VIDEO STUDY
978-1-62405-209-5

KINGDOM MARRIAGE
978-1-58997-820-1

KINGDOM MARRIAGE
DEVOTIONAL
978-1-58997-856-0

KINGDOM MARRIAGE
VIDEO STUDY
978-1-58997-834-8

RAISING KINGDOM KIDS
978-1-58997-784-6

RAISING KINGDOM KIDS
DEVOTIONAL
978-1-62405-409-9

RAISING KINGDOM KIDS
VIDEO STUDY
978-1-62405-407-5

KINGDOM FAMILY
DEVOTIONAL
978-1-58997-855-3

CP0845